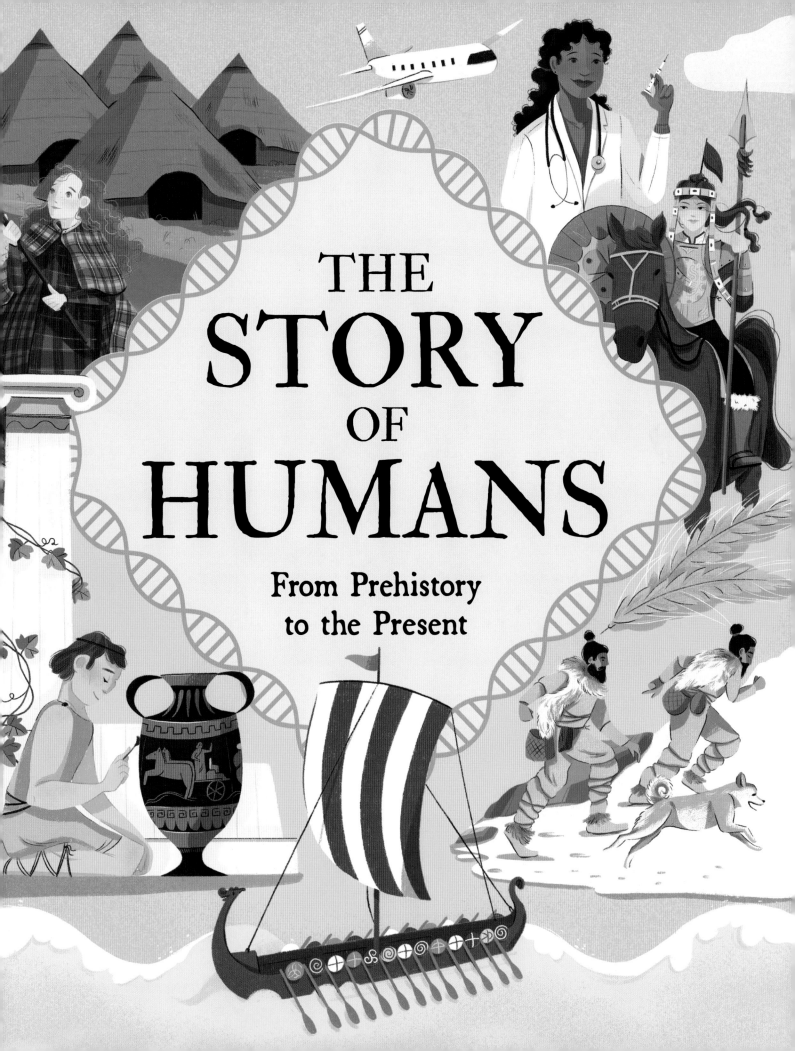

THE STORY OF HUMANS

From Prehistory to the Present

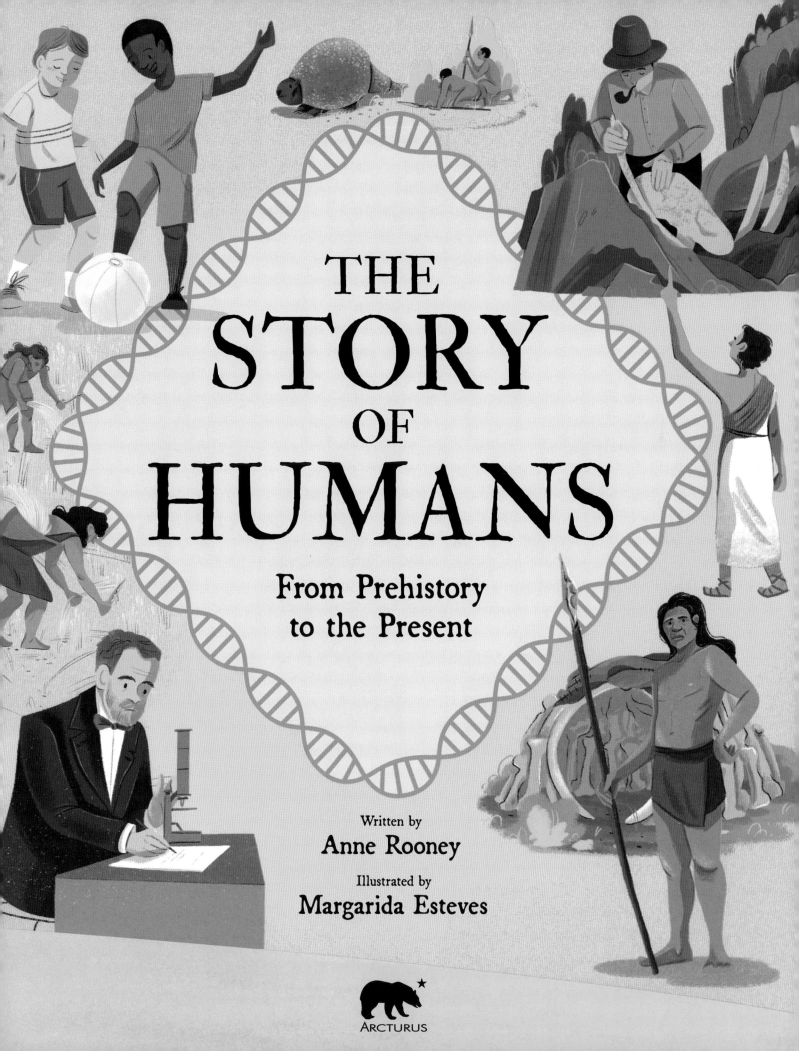

THE STORY OF HUMANS

From Prehistory to the Present

Written by
Anne Rooney

Illustrated by
Margarida Esteves

ARCTURUS

ARCTURUS

This edition published in 2023 by
Arcturus Publishing Limited
26/27 Bickels Yard,
151–153 Bermondsey Street,
London SW1 3HA

Author: Anne Rooney
Illustrator: Margarida Esteves
Designer: Sally Bond
Editor: Donna Gregory
Design Manager: Jessica Holliland
Editorial Manager: Joe Harris

ISBN: 978-1-3988-2021-0
CH007801NT

Supplier 29, Date 0822, PI 00001001

Printed in Singapore

CONTENTS

INTRODUCTION

Earth has been here for 4.5 billion years—but humans have been on Earth for only a brief moment in the planet's history. If the history of Earth was squashed into one year, humans would arrive in the final hour of December 31. There has been life on land for only 400 million years—less than the last half billion years. Modern humans, *Homo sapiens*, evolved only 300,000 years ago, and our lives have changed rapidly over only the last 10,000 years.

One of our very earliest ancestors is the tiny *Plesiadapis*, a rodent-like mammal from approximately 55 million years ago.

Stories of starting out

The fossils of early humans were first found in the nineteenth century, and the theory of evolution dates from the same period. Before that, people who wondered where humans first came from made up stories to explain our presence on Earth. These became myths and religions, told in many different versions around the world. For example, a Santali myth from India tells that Earth was originally entirely water, then the land was made by an earthworm depositing soil on the back of a turtle. The god Marang Buru had created two swans, which went to live on the land. The female swam laid two eggs, from which the first humans hatched. They were named Pilchu Haram and Pilchu Budhi, and became the ancestors of the whole human race.

The science of humankind

We now know that humans, like all other living things on Earth, have evolved over a very long period of time from previous living organisms. The origins of life lie in the deep past—at least 3.5 billion years ago. Over that time, organisms evolved different features that suited them to different environments and ways of living. Humans are no different from tigers, or trees, or sponges in this regard.

Our human ancestors evolved first to live in the forests and plains of Africa over two million years ago. Since then, we have adapted to living all around the world. Our bodies have changed a little to suit different climates and living conditions. People whose ancestors lived near the equator have darker skin, which protected them from sunburn and skin cancers. This was how all people looked to start with. People who lived where there was less intense sunlight evolved lighter skin. With weaker sunlight, their bodies needed to make the most of it to produce essential vitamin D. They couldn't afford to block light with dark skin. Pale skin is a recent development—perhaps less than 10,000 years old.

Homo habilis (left) was the first human species known to make stone tools, starting out on the path to modern humans.

A Note About Dates

Some of the events in this book happened a very long time ago. They are given dates in the form of millions of years ago (mya) or thousands of years ago (counting backward from now). From 12,000 years ago, dates are given the labels BCE (Before Common Era) or CE (Common Era). The Common Era started around 2,000 years ago–it's where we count our current dates from. The date 10,000 BCE is 12,000 years ago.

Paranthropus (left) lived 2.7–2.3 million years ago, overlapping with the earliest human (*Homo*) species such as *Homo habilis* (top).

Fast forward

We have gone beyond other animals in learning to change the world to suit ourselves, rather than always having to change ourselves to suit the world. This means we have been able to move to new environments and adapt much more quickly than other organisms. People could move into cold regions as soon as they could start fires and make simple clothes from animal skins. Once they began to farm animals and crops, they built larger communities which became cities. Civilizations then grew quickly, bringing more and more new developments at an ever-increasing pace. In our modern world, many people have little contact with the natural world. We don't hunt for, or even grow, our own food. Our lives are unimaginably different from those of our ancestors even just a few thousand years ago.

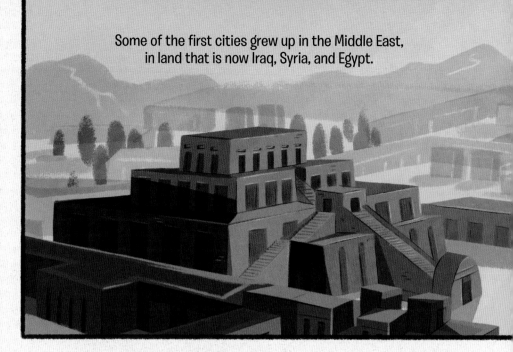

Some of the first cities grew up in the Middle East, in land that is now Iraq, Syria, and Egypt.

Life's not a competition

Civilizations emerged around the world independently, in places that had no communication with each other. On opposite sides of vast oceans, where people had no idea there were other humans elsewhere, people separately developed agriculture, clothes, wheels, art, writing, astronomy, metalworking, pottery, and much else. These developments happened at different times according to the needs and resources of different groups.

Some developments didn't happen everywhere. People in South America didn't use wheels for transportation, for example, because they had no animals that could pull carts, and their land was mountainous. Some cultures had no written language, so we have no detailed record of their achievements or thoughts. It doesn't mean that they were less advanced, cultured, or intelligent than any other people—we just lack evidence of what they did.

Vikings crossed the sea from Europe to Greenland 1,000 years ago.

People who have lived in the frozen north of America, Asia, and Europe often made their houses from ice and left no writing or metal tools, so we know little about their early culture.

One world

People around the world have similar abilities and brains. Different regions have been at the forefront of advances at different times. This was sometimes because the challenges of their environment forced people in a particular place to find solutions to problems. Sometimes it was the opposite—better conditions gave them time and resources for invention, exploration, deep thought, and experimentation. The Middle East, North Africa, India, China, and Europe have all been at the forefront of new developments at different times in history and prehistory. No culture owns or has a monopoly on advances; they are the property and inheritance of all humankind.

Chinese knife money, used in trading.

In the last century, humans have pushed beyond Earth to begin exploring space not just with telescopes but in person and with robotic craft. The story of humans began on Earth, but who knows where it may go next?

Apollo Moon landing, 1969.

BEFORE US

Humans need a home—and our home is Earth, a blue planet whirling around the Sun with seven others. It has taken four-and-a-half billion years for Earth—and humans—to get where we are now.

Earth began in a cloud of dust, gas, and ice circling the early sun. As fragments of dust and ice crashed into each other, they stuck together, growing into larger and larger lumps and eventually making eight planets and lots of leftover chunks. In the molten early Earth, gravity pulled heavier metals to the middle, while lighter rock and gases rose to the surface. The outside slowly cooled and hardened as heat escaped into space. Eruptions of molten rock from below often split the new surface with long, fiery gashes. These belched out clouds of gas and vaporized water that cloaked the surface, making an early atmosphere. Rain fell for millions of years, making a vast ocean. At last, the planet was ready for life.

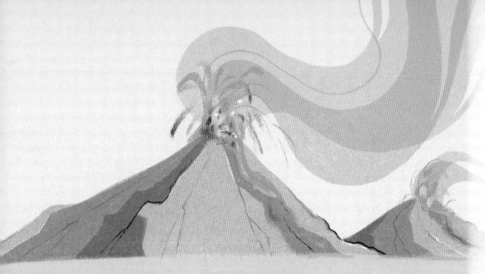

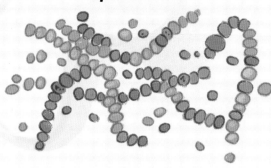

Cyanobacteria

LIFE BEGINS

No one knows exactly how or where life began on Earth, but it was probably in water between 3.4 and 4.1 billion years ago. Perhaps it started in a warm pool on the surface, a shallow sea, or even a deep-sea vent—an opening in the seabed that pours out mineral-rich hot water. The first living things were tiny, single-celled microbes, possibly similar to the bacteria and archea that still live today.

A breath of fresh air

Earth's early atmosphere was mostly carbon dioxide and nitrogen. The first microbes used carbon-based chemicals in the water to fuel their tiny bodies. Then, at some time between 3.6 and 2.7 billion years ago, some microbes called cyanobacteria began to do things differently. They started making sugars from water and carbon dioxide using the energy from sunlight as green plants do now. This produced oxygen. The cyanobacteria were very successful and poured out so much oxygen that it dissolved in seawater and changed the rocks. Eventually, oxygen began to escape into the atmosphere, causing the "Great Oxygenation Event" around 2.4 billion years ago. This was the start of our modern oxygen-rich atmosphere.

Frozen Earth

Without atmospheric oxygen, we wouldn't be here, but at the time it was catastrophic. Carbon dioxide is a greenhouse gas and holds heat close to Earth, keeping it warm. The cyanobacteria removed some of the carbon dioxide from the air. This cooled the planet so much that ice spread over the entire surface, turning Earth into a giant snowball for hundreds of millions of years.

Life on hold

While Earth was frozen, microbes clung to life under the ice or in little pockets of liquid water. Slowly, volcanoes added carbon dioxide back into the atmosphere, eventually warming the planet enough to melt the ice. Life took a new direction in the thaw.

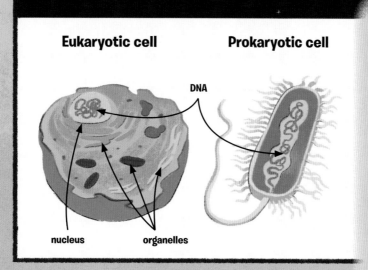

Eukaryotic cell   **Prokaryotic cell**

DNA

nucleus   organelles

Bangiomorpha

Bangiomorpha, a type of red algae, is an early multicelled organism. It lived one billion years ago.

One and then more

While early microbes sometimes grouped together in long strings or layers called microbial mats, the cells were all the same. But around a billion years ago, cells began to group together and change, with different cells taking on different tasks in the first multicelled organisms. The cells that did this were more complex than others. Called eukaryotic cells, they had a nucleus to hold their genetic material and separate parts, called organelles, to perform different tasks in the cell. The earlier type, prokaryotic cells, remained simple. Today, there are still both types of cells. All multicelled organisms, including plants and animals, have eukaryotic cells. Many microbes are prokaryotic.

AN EXPLOSION OF LIFE

Some multicelled organisms developed sexual reproduction. *Bangiomorpha* is the earliest known to do this. It meant that each new organism had two parents and a mix of features from each. Before this, all organisms were an exact copy of one parent, produced by asexual reproduction. Mixing features from two parents meant that evolution—changes in organisms—could take place much more quickly.

Understanding evolution

When an organism reproduces, the genetic information that acts as a "recipe" for it is copied. Organisms that are well suited to their environment and live to reproduce, pass on their genetic information to the next generation. Those that are less well suited might not survive and reproduce. A mistake copying the genetic code is called a mutation. Some mutations help organisms, some are harmful, and most make no difference. Helpful mutations tend to survive and pass on their genes. Over many generations, the usual features of an organism can change. This is called evolution.

From simple to complex

The first multicelled organisms were probably similar to sponges, with just a few different types of cells and a simple body structure. They were soft-bodied and couldn't move around. After more Snowball Earth events, from 715 to 600 million years ago, multicelled organisms really took off, rapidly becoming larger and more complex.

Around 600 million years ago, the first animals roamed over the seabed feeding on mat-like layers of microbes. Unlike earlier organisms, they were symmetrical, and had different top and bottom sides. This was the Ediacaran, the first era of animals.

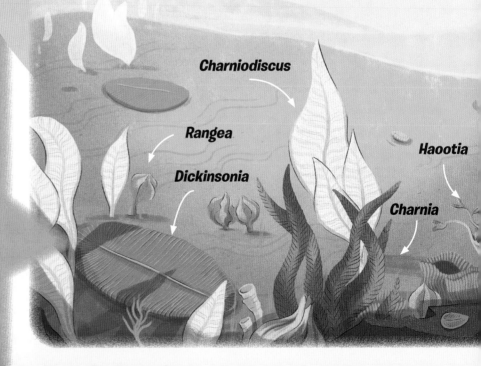

Ediacaran seabed, around 600 million years ago

Charniodiscus

Rangea

Dickinsonia

Haootia

Charnia

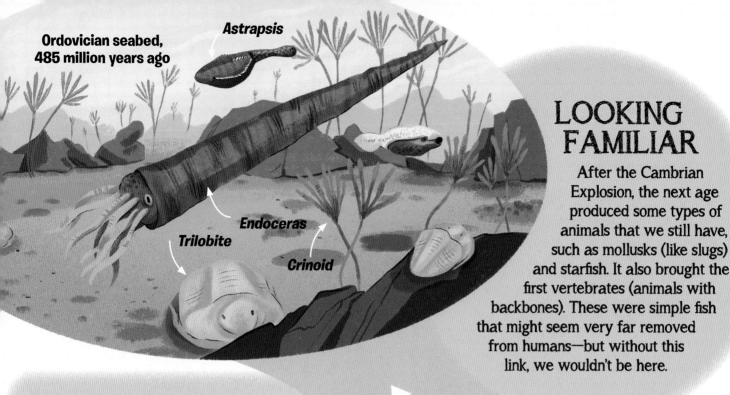

Ordovician seabed, 485 million years ago

Astrapsis

Endoceras

Trilobite

Crinoid

LOOKING FAMILIAR

After the Cambrian Explosion, the next age produced some types of animals that we still have, such as mollusks (like slugs) and starfish. It also brought the first vertebrates (animals with backbones). These were simple fish that might seem very far removed from humans—but without this link, we wouldn't be here.

The Ediacaran was followed 541 million years ago by the so-called "Cambrian Explosion" when life diversified (became different) very quickly. Eyes evolved, and as animals began to eat each other, they developed ways of moving quickly to chase or escape from others. Prey evolved ways of defending themselves, like a hard outside, and predators evolved ways to crunch through hard outsides. The first large collections of fossils are from this time as the hard parts of animals fossilize much more easily than soft parts.

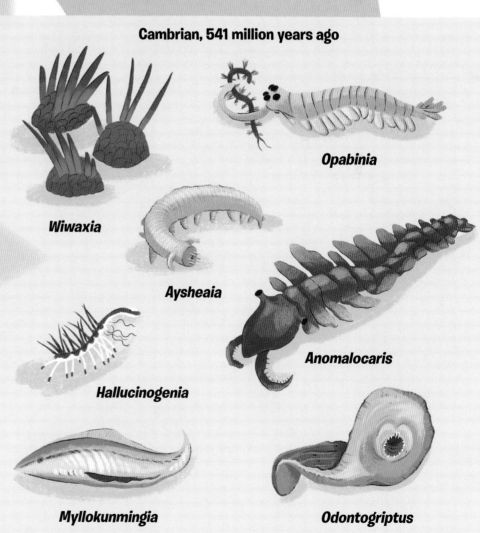

Cambrian, 541 million years ago

Wiwaxia

Opabinia

Aysheaia

Hallucinogenia

Anomalocaris

Myllokunmingia

Odontogriptus

CLAIMING THE LAND

Fish might seem a poor start to life on land, but it was from those first vertebrates that our earliest land-going ancestors evolved. Until 400 million years ago, almost all life was in the sea. But then another change in the atmosphere made life on land possible. A layer of the gas ozone collected at the top of the atmosphere, which kept out harmful radiation from the Sun. Soon, plants, fungi, and animals took advantage of the change and moved ashore.

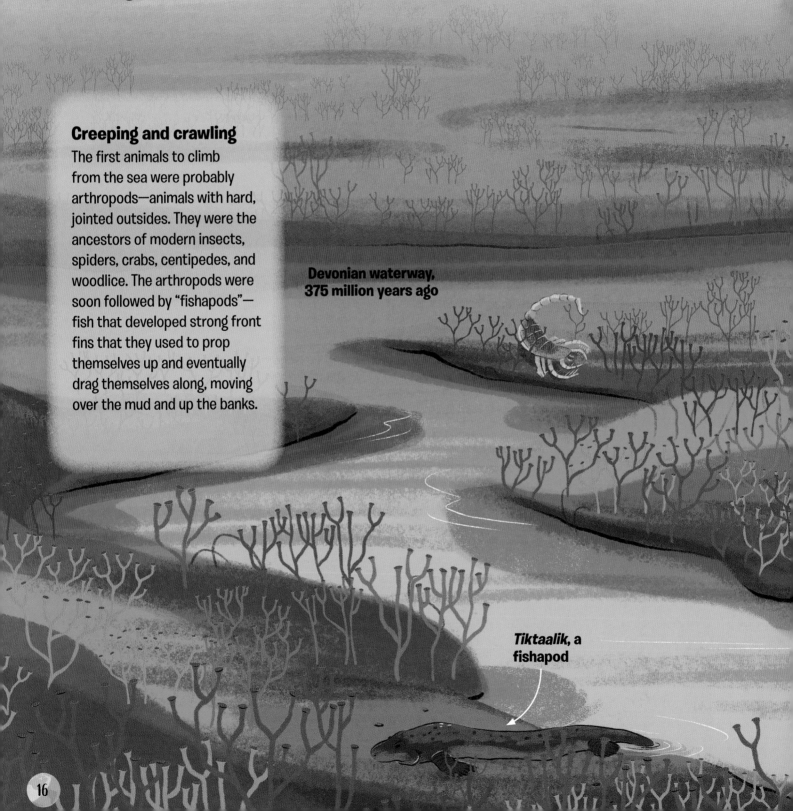

Creeping and crawling

The first animals to climb from the sea were probably arthropods—animals with hard, jointed outsides. They were the ancestors of modern insects, spiders, crabs, centipedes, and woodlice. The arthropods were soon followed by "fishapods"— fish that developed strong front fins that they used to prop themselves up and eventually drag themselves along, moving over the mud and up the banks.

Devonian waterway, 375 million years ago

Tiktaalik, a fishapod

Four feet are better than none

Fish have no feet, but quadrupeds—four-footed animals—evolved from them. Fishapods developed from lobe-finned fish: fish that had thick, fleshy lobes at the top of the fins where they attached to the body. These lobes were well suited to evolving into limbs. The strong, front, prop-like fins became front legs, and fins at the back became back legs. The oldest fossilized tracks left by a quadruped on land were made 397 million years ago. From the early quadrupeds, all modern amphibians, reptiles, birds, and mammals have evolved—including humans. All these have four limbs, whether they are legs, arms, or wings, except for a few that have lost them, such as snakes.

Follow the water

At first, animals followed waterways inland, so life was near rivers and swamps. Amphibians evolved from the fishapods. Modern amphibians include frogs and salamanders. Even today, amphibians need to lay their eggs in water, and their young live in water. Early amphibians grew to huge sizes, and lived in the warm swamps.

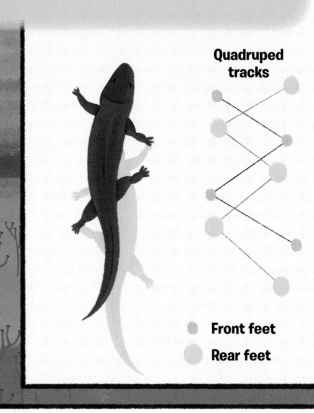

Quadruped tracks

● Front feet
● Rear feet

Free to roam

Squashy eggs that need to stay in water limited where amphibians could live. In time, reptiles evolved from them that overcame this problem. They laid eggs with a tough, leathery, or hard outside. Water could not escape through the shell, so the eggs could survive on land without drying out. This freed the reptiles to move farther inland and live on all parts of the land. They grew to huge sizes and included both plant-eaters (herbivores) and meat-eaters (carnivores),

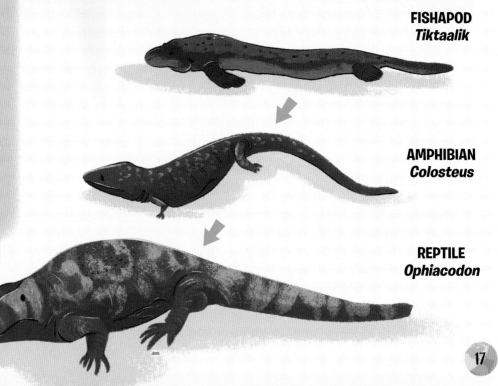

FISHAPOD
Tiktaalik

AMPHIBIAN
Colosteus

REPTILE
Ophiacodon

TOWARD MAMMALS

The reptiles thrived in a period when much of Earth was cloaked in lush, dense forest and hot swamps. This was the Carboniferous, 359–299 million years ago. Trees poured oxygen into the atmosphere, and the planet heated up. Some animals grew to huge sizes, including giant insects and other arthropods. In this tropical landscape, a group of reptiles called pelycosaurs set out on the path to becoming mammals—but there was still a long way to go.

Meganeura

Reptiles like mammals

Unlike their more typically reptilian ancestors, pelycosaurs had no scales, but a mix of bony plates called "osteoderms" and bare skin on different parts of the body. Like later mammals, including us, they grew different types of teeth, while a reptile has teeth of only one type but different sizes. Some pelycosaurs, like *Dimetrodon*, had a large sail of skin on the back, probably used to control its temperature or to attract a mate. Although some of these look something like later dinosaurs, dinosaurs evolved from a different line of reptiles.

Procynosuchus was a reptile on the way to becoming a mammal—but also on the way back into the water. It probably lived somewhat like a modern otter, hunting fish but also able to go on land.

Procynosuchus—a cynodont
about 60 cm (2 ft) long

The pelycosaur **Ophiacodon** lived in North America 290 million years ago. A strong, meat-eating predator, it grew up to 3 m (10 ft) long.

Dimetrodon

The pelycosaurs gave rise to therapsids, which were a bit more like mammals. They had three different types of teeth, which we have now—incisors for nipping, canines for puncturing and tearing, and molars for chewing. They were probably warm-blooded, and at least some of them had hair or fur. A group of therapsids called cynodonts emerged around 200 million years ago. All modern mammals, including humans, are cynodonts. But before true mammals could evolve, our strange ancestors had to survive the greatest catastrophe life on Earth has ever seen.

Life's great reset

The Permian period ended 252 million years ago with a devastating mass extinction event known as the "Great Dying." It's an appropriate name—more than 90 percent of all species on Earth died out. The catastrophe was caused by thousands of years of violent volcanic eruptions that poured carbon dioxide into the atmosphere and pushed up temperatures by 8°C (14°F). The devastation lasted millions of years, yet a few animals survived, probably by digging burrows to escape the worst of the catastrophe's impact.

The pig-sized **Lystrosaurus** survived remarkably well. Around 95 percent of the vertebrate fossils found after the Great Dying in some places are of *Lystrosaurus*.

DOWN AMONG THE DINOSAURS

It took a long time—perhaps ten million years—for the world to settle down and for life to match the levels seen before the Great Dying. In this period, called the Triassic, some reptiles evolved into the dinosaurs. The surviving cynodonts became more like mammals.

First mammals

The first true mammals appeared over 225 million years ago in different parts of the world. They were generally small and kept out of the way of larger animals, including dinosaurs, that might eat them or even step on them. Many mammals were probably nocturnal, coming out only at night when it was safer, and sheltered in burrows or trees during the more dangerous daylight hours.

Agilodocodon scampered through the trees, probably using its tail to help it balance.

Anchiornis

Castorocauda was one of the larger early mammals at around 50 cm (2 ft) long. Like a modern beaver or otter, it spent most of its time in the water.

Eating plants and eating meat

The cynodonts split into two main groups. One group mostly ate plants, and the other mostly ate meat. Twenty-five million years after the Great Dying, some of the meat-eating group became the first mammals, their bodies changing. Some bones in the lower jaw moved to the ear, becoming part of the hearing system. They grew fur, began to give birth to live babies, and produced milk to feed their babies.

PELYCOSAUR
Dimetrodon

THERAPSID
Lystrosaurus

MAMMAL
Morganucodon

Just 6 cm (2 in) long, the tiny **Microdocodon** probably ate insects.

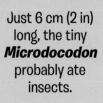

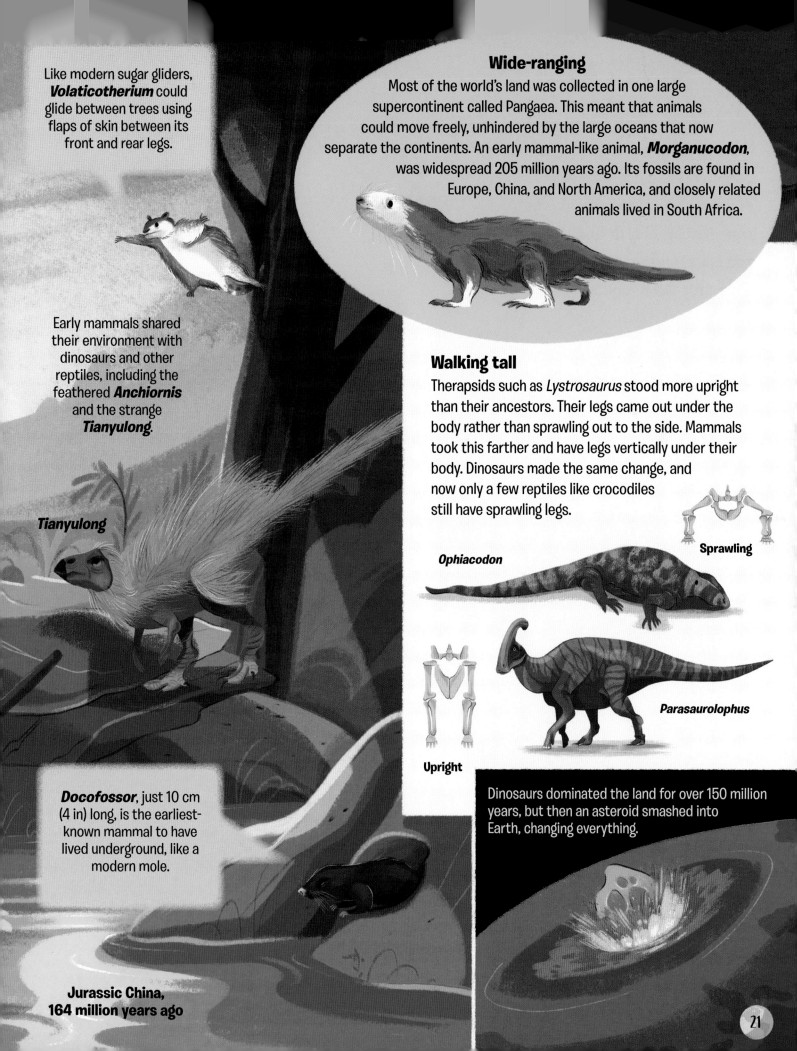

Like modern sugar gliders, **Volaticotherium** could glide between trees using flaps of skin between its front and rear legs.

Wide-ranging

Most of the world's land was collected in one large supercontinent called Pangaea. This meant that animals could move freely, unhindered by the large oceans that now separate the continents. An early mammal-like animal, **Morganucodon**, was widespread 205 million years ago. Its fossils are found in Europe, China, and North America, and closely related animals lived in South Africa.

Early mammals shared their environment with dinosaurs and other reptiles, including the feathered **Anchiornis** and the strange **Tianyulong**.

Tianyulong

Walking tall

Therapsids such as *Lystrosaurus* stood more upright than their ancestors. Their legs came out under the body rather than sprawling out to the side. Mammals took this farther and have legs vertically under their body. Dinosaurs made the same change, and now only a few reptiles like crocodiles still have sprawling legs.

Ophiacodon

Sprawling

Parasaurolophus

Upright

Docofossor, just 10 cm (4 in) long, is the earliest-known mammal to have lived underground, like a modern mole.

Dinosaurs dominated the land for over 150 million years, but then an asteroid smashed into Earth, changing everything.

Jurassic China, 164 million years ago

IN AND OUT OF THE TREES

Mammals appeared after one worldwide catastrophe and grew more successful after another. The asteroid that smashed into Earth 65.5 million years ago killed all the non-bird dinosaurs. That left space for the mammals to take over.

Tetonius lived 54 million years ago. Its large eyes show that it was active at night.

43 mya

Our branch of the tree

The mammals that survived the death of the dinosaurs were small, but soon grew larger and started to live in different ways. Among them, a group of rodent-like animals living in the trees became the primates. All apes and monkeys—including humans—are primates.

Plesiadapis was an ancestor of primates. It probably spent a lot of time in trees, since its hands and feet were suited to grasping branches.

Tiny *Archicebus*, about the size of a mouse, is the oldest-known primate. It had features of both monkeys and apes

The world of the primates

Fifty million years ago, tropical forest covered much of the world. The primates shared it with many other kinds of animals.

As grasslands spread and changed, large grazing mammals like *Uintatherium* evolved.

Gastornis was a giant, flightless bird. Although over 2 m (6 ft 6 in) tall, it ate only plants and fruit.

Phenacodus was an early hoofed mammal that lived in North America.

Carnivores such as the vicious *Hyaenodon* preyed on the grazers.

56 mya

45 mya

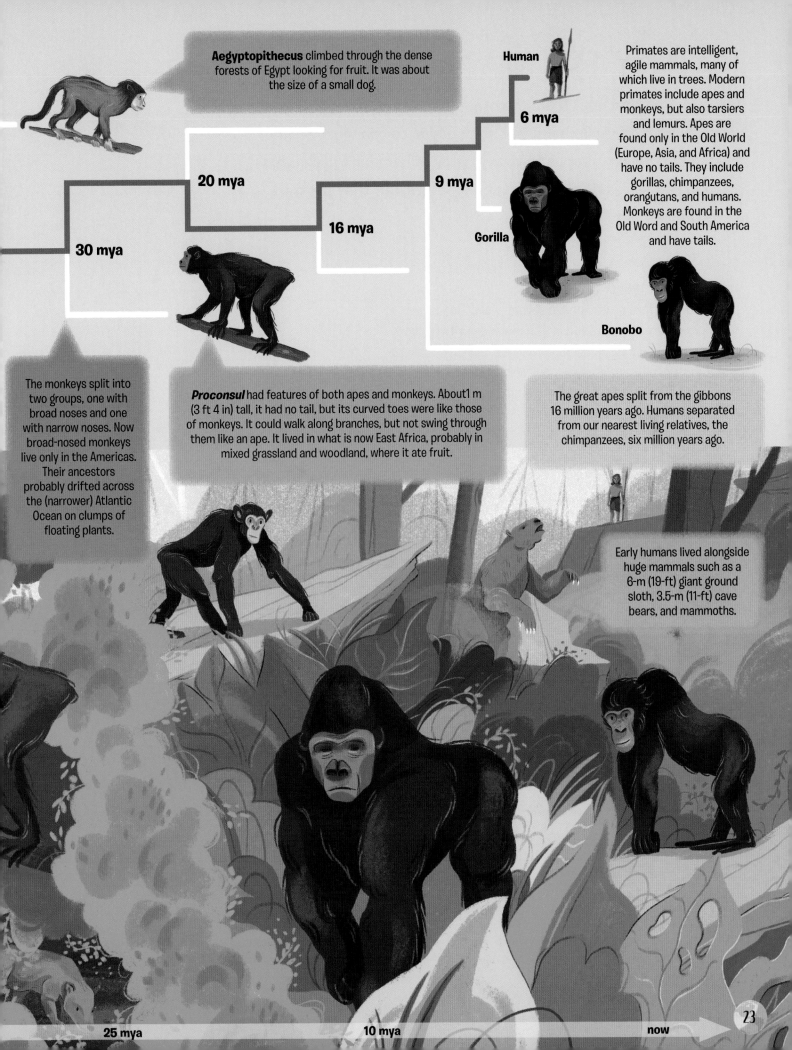

Aegyptopithecus climbed through the dense forests of Egypt looking for fruit. It was about the size of a small dog.

Human

6 mya

20 mya

16 mya

9 mya

30 mya

Gorilla

Bonobo

Primates are intelligent, agile mammals, many of which live in trees. Modern primates include apes and monkeys, but also tarsiers and lemurs. Apes are found only in the Old World (Europe, Asia, and Africa) and have no tails. They include gorillas, chimpanzees, orangutans, and humans. Monkeys are found in the Old Word and South America and have tails.

The monkeys split into two groups, one with broad noses and one with narrow noses. Now broad-nosed monkeys live only in the Americas. Their ancestors probably drifted across the (narrower) Atlantic Ocean on clumps of floating plants.

Proconsul had features of both apes and monkeys. About 1 m (3 ft 4 in) tall, it had no tail, but its curved toes were like those of monkeys. It could walk along branches, but not swing through them like an ape. It lived in what is now East Africa, probably in mixed grassland and woodland, where it ate fruit.

The great apes split from the gibbons 16 million years ago. Humans separated from our nearest living relatives, the chimpanzees, six million years ago.

Early humans lived alongside huge mammals such as a 6-m (19-ft) giant ground sloth, 3.5-m (11-ft) cave bears, and mammoths.

EARLY HUMAN FAMILY

The primates that split from the other great apes six million years ago were unlike modern humans, but soon began to change. Between six and two million years ago, many types of humanlike primates evolved. They are not all our direct ancestors, but they are part of the human family.

Climbing and walking

Humans differ from other apes in several ways. One is our feet. Chimpanzees have feet a little like hands, with a clearly separated big toe that can grasp branches. Our own toes are all in a line, unsuited to grasping, but perfect for walking on the ground. Gorillas have feet in between those of humans and chimpanzees.

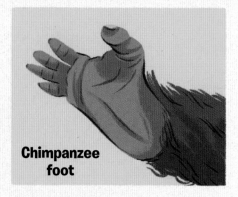

Chimpanzee foot

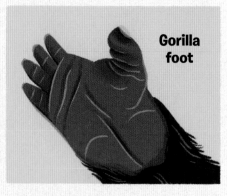

Gorilla foot

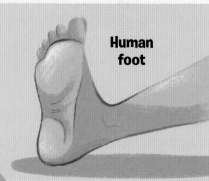

Human foot

3.
Paranthropus lived 2.7–2.3 million years ago, overlapping with early humans. They might have used fire and probably used bones as tools. They chose the same types of bones repeatedly, perhaps selecting those suitable for a particular task.

1.
Ardipithecus lived in Africa 7–4 million years ago. Well adapted to walking on two legs, they also climbed trees.

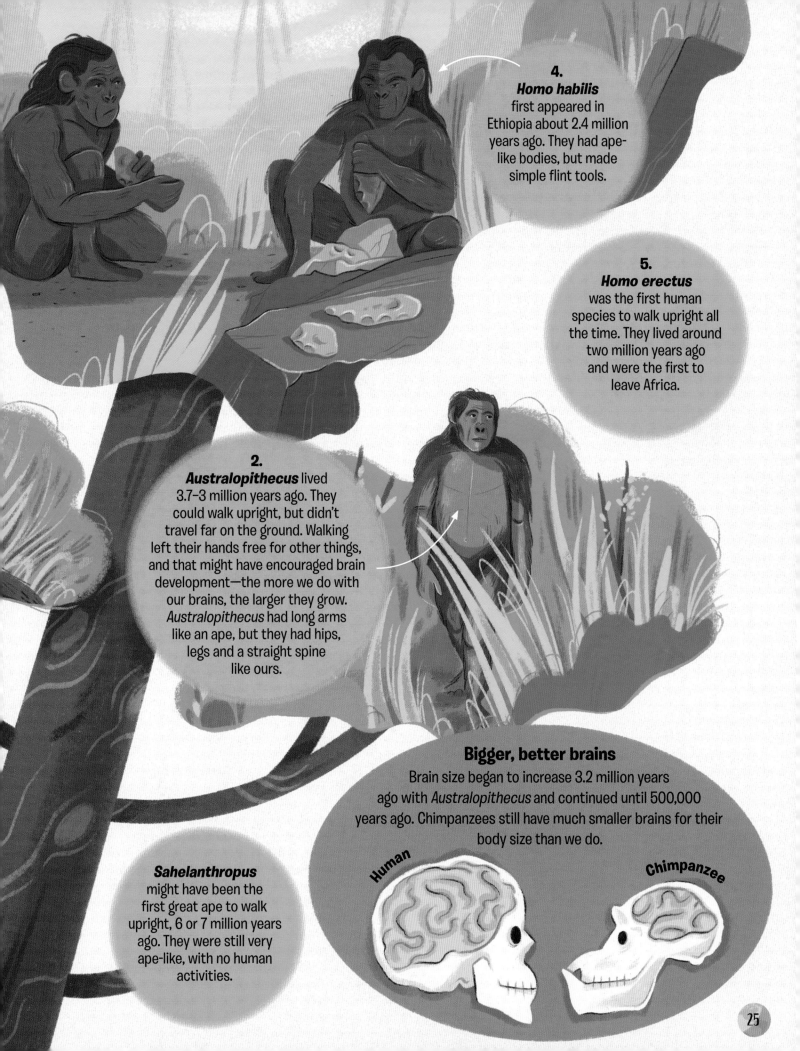

4.
Homo habilis
first appeared in Ethiopia about 2.4 million years ago. They had ape-like bodies, but made simple flint tools.

5.
Homo erectus
was the first human species to walk upright all the time. They lived around two million years ago and were the first to leave Africa.

2.
Australopithecus lived 3.7–3 million years ago. They could walk upright, but didn't travel far on the ground. Walking left their hands free for other things, and that might have encouraged brain development—the more we do with our brains, the larger they grow. *Australopithecus* had long arms like an ape, but they had hips, legs and a straight spine like ours.

Bigger, better brains
Brain size began to increase 3.2 million years ago with *Australopithecus* and continued until 500,000 years ago. Chimpanzees still have much smaller brains for their body size than we do.

Human

Chimpanzee

Sahelanthropus
might have been the first great ape to walk upright, 6 or 7 million years ago. They were still very ape-like, with no human activities.

Homo heidelbergensis emerged 1.3 million years ago and entered Europe 500,000 years ago. They could control fire and were the first to make shelters, use wooden spears, and hunt large animals.

Neanderthals, or **Homo neanderthalensis**, lived in Europe and Asia from 400,000 years ago. They sometimes lived alongside *Homo sapiens*. They made sophisticated tools, built shelters, made clothes, made art, buried their dead, and probably used language. No one knows why they died out, but most were gone by around 40,000 years ago.

Europe

Asia

Homo habilis was the first *Homo* species, living 2.4–1.4 million years ago in Africa. They were shorter than us, hairy, and probably still lived partly in the trees—as did **Australopithecus**. They used simple stone tools and ate meat, which they probably scavenged.

Africa

Homo naledi survived until at least 300,000 years ago in Africa, yet still had some primitive features and a small brain.

The eruption of Toba, in Indonesia, 75,000 years ago, caused local devastation and widespread climate change.

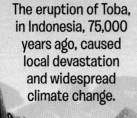

Modern humans, **Homo sapiens**, evolved in Africa around 350,000–400,000 years ago and left the continent between 70,000 and 50,000 years ago.

Humans didn't leave Africa and stay away. Some moved back into Africa, and modern humans evolved from some of these.

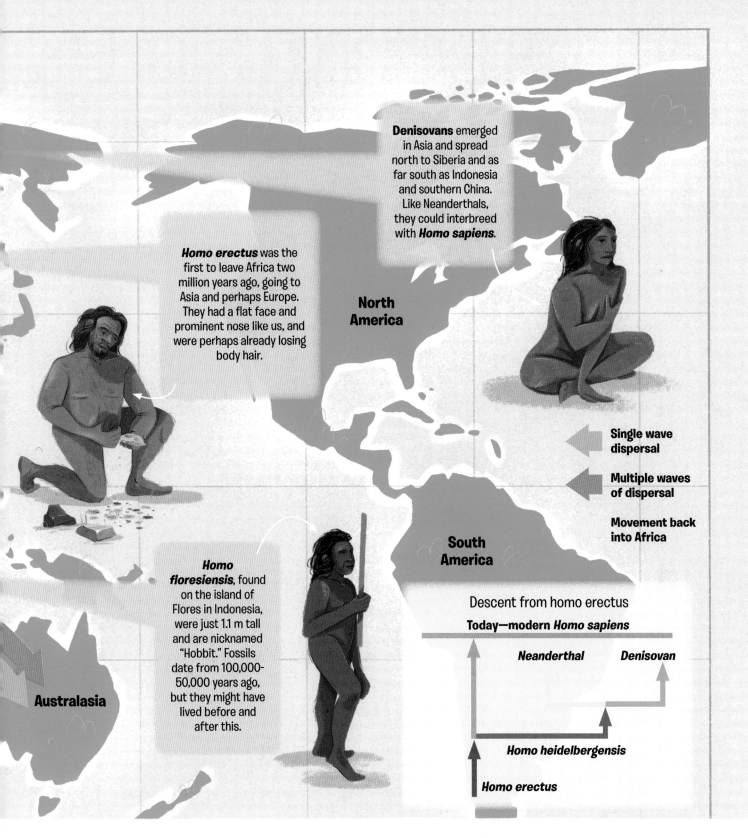

Denisovans emerged in Asia and spread north to Siberia and as far south as Indonesia and southern China. Like Neanderthals, they could interbreed with *Homo sapiens*.

Homo erectus was the first to leave Africa two million years ago, going to Asia and perhaps Europe. They had a flat face and prominent nose like us, and were perhaps already losing body hair.

North America

Single wave dispersal

Multiple waves of dispersal

Movement back into Africa

Homo floresiensis, found on the island of Flores in Indonesia, were just 1.1 m tall and are nicknamed "Hobbit." Fossils date from 100,000–50,000 years ago, but they might have lived before and after this.

South America

Australasia

Descent from homo erectus

Today—modern *Homo sapiens*

Neanderthal   *Denisovan*

Homo heidelbergensis

Homo erectus

BROTHERS, SISTERS, AND COUSINS

There have been at least 20 different species of *Homo*, or humans, of which we are the only survivors. Some are on separate branches of the evolutionary tree, as cousins, brothers, or sisters to modern humans. Humans began in Africa and spread around the world, changing as they went to suit the environments they lived in.

BECOMING US

We think of ourselves as "human" because of the things we do that other animals don't do, such as using language, tools, and fire, making art, burying our dead, and having an internal life of thoughts, feelings, hopes, and plans. Many of these activities began with the larger human family of our early ancestors.

Humans were first hunter-gatherers, following the animals they hunted as they migrated and moving with seasonal changes in the plants they ate. Over a period of around 2.5 million years, they began to make tools from stone, bone, and wood, to tame fire and cook food, to fashion shelters and clothing. The older Stone Age, called the Paleolithic, began with the first use of stone tools, around 3.3 million years ago. It lasted until 10,000 BCE (12,000 years ago), when humans began to settle and farm the land.

HANDY HUMANS AND THEIR TOOLS

Many animals use an object they find as a tool for an immediate task. The earliest known stone tools are 3.3 million years old, and were perhaps used by *Australopithecus*. But early humans went beyond using stones they found as tools and began to make tools for a particular purpose. This took more than just physical skill. They had to imagine a tool that did not yet exist, think ahead, see how to change an item to make it useful, and then know how to shape the stone to make the tool they wanted.

The name *Homo habilis* means "handy man" and is the name given to the first humans who are known to have made tools.

Homo erectus

Modern humans have less body hair than other apes or earlier types of human. They might have started losing hair as they began to use fire to keep warm.

Knocking and knapping

Experts divide early stone tools into three types. The first type, or Mode 1 tools, were first made in Africa 2.6 million years ago–a little before the earliest *Homo habilis* fossils. These tools have a simple shape and were made using a large, rounded stone called a hammerstone to chip flakes off a smaller "core" stone. The sharp-edged flakes were used for cutting and scraping, and the sharpened core could be used as a chopper. Knocking off flakes of stone is called "knapping".

Two faced

Mode 2 tools were more carefully cut to have two shaped faces. Many were oval or pear-shaped hand axes. While the sharp flakes of flint knocked off the core stone were most important for the earliest tool-makers, Mode 2 tool-makers focused on the core itself. They shaped it first by knocking off large flakes with a hammerstone, and then removing smaller flakes symmetrically, often using tools made of bone or antler. Mode 2 tools first appeared 1.7 million years ago and were made until just 130,000 years ago.

Finest grade

The third type of stone tools, Mode 3, were first made in Africa 315,000 years ago. They were finely worked by *Homo sapiens* and Neanderthals, and made into thin, sharp items. These included spearheads, arrowheads, scrapers for working leather, and sharp stones used for scratching or carving on other objects.

SEW COOL

The tools people made depended on their needs and what was available. People started to make bone needles 35,000 years ago. They were especially useful in Ice-Age Europe and Russia, as making clothes from animal skins allowed people to move into lands that were otherwise too cold.

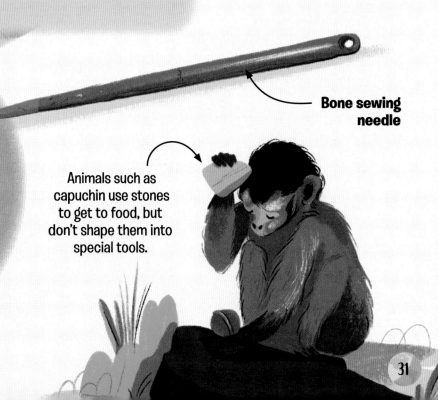

Bone sewing needle

Animals such as capuchin use stones to get to food, but don't shape them into special tools.

31

Fire could be used to frighten away predators.

FIRE!

Using fire set humans apart from other animals. People probably began by capturing fires that had started naturally (wildfires) and keeping them alight as long possible. Later, they learned to kindle fire from sparks made by striking flints together or by turning hardwood against softwood to create heat.

Hot spots

Fires start naturally when lightning strikes dry, wooded areas or dry grass. Today, people flee from wildfires, which are very dangerous. Our distant ancestors might have welcomed them, at least sometimes. A wildfire kills animals that can be scavenged and eaten. It leaves small pockets of burning fire that could be trapped and kept going. Early humans might have cooked food in hotspots or found partly charred animal carcasses to eat. Maybe they carried burning branches to a more convenient place and built a hearth of stones to contain a fire and keep it burning.

Firing up

Taming fire changed the lives of early humans. Fire gave light and heat, so people could stay active into the night and could live in colder areas. Wood and stone tempered in fire make harder tools, leading to more successful hunts and so more food. People in Germany made fire-hardened wooden spears 400,000 years ago, and in South Africa stone changed by fire was knapped into curved blades. Fire could be used to clear land and to clean out caves for living in.

Fire was also vital for cooking. Cooked meat is easier to eat and digest than raw meat, so people could eat more, gaining more energy. Cooking kills parasites and bacteria. Cooking food even changed our bodies—softer food led to reduced jaw size and a shorter gut. Better nutrition led to bigger brains and increased populations.

Millions of years of fire

People might have used fire two million years ago, but the first certain evidence is a million years old, from *Homo erectus*. A cave in South Africa has tiny bits of wood ash alongside burned animal bones and stone tools. By 200,000 years ago, hearths were widespread in Europe and the Middle East. Before that, fire might have been used only irregularly and not necessarily for cooking meat.

Using a bow drill to make fire

Fire-hardened spear tip

Sitting around the fire in the evening possibly helped the development of language.

HOME FROM HOME

Humans evolved after some primates came down from the trees and spent more time on the ground, walking upright all the time and venturing into open grassland. *Homo erectus* was the first group, or among the first, to follow this more "human" lifestyle. They must have given up sleeping in the trees and begun seeking shelter on the ground.

A cave gave shelter from the weather and from wild animals.

Cavemen and cavewomen?

Early humans first sheltered in safe spaces they found, such as caves. A cave in the Kalahari desert in South Africa was used by early humans such as *Homo habilis* or *Homo erectus* two million years ago. We know that people lived in caves because many of their objects have been found there. They lit fires in hearths, dropped pieces of knapped flint, and left behind pieces of bone from their meals. They even began to decorate the walls of the caves they lived in with drawings and handprints. A cave in Indonesia has a painting of a pig made at least 45,500 years ago. Some groups possibly moved between caves in a regular pattern as they followed the animals they hunted, migrating over the same routes year after year.

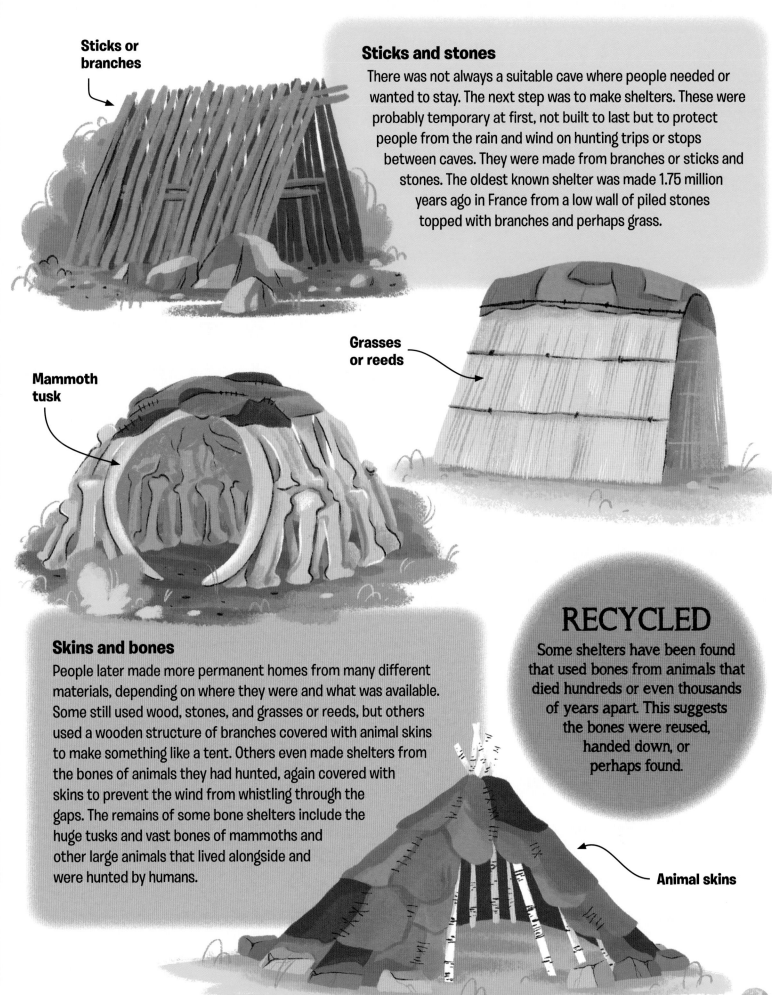

Sticks or branches

Sticks and stones

There was not always a suitable cave where people needed or wanted to stay. The next step was to make shelters. These were probably temporary at first, not built to last but to protect people from the rain and wind on hunting trips or stops between caves. They were made from branches or sticks and stones. The oldest known shelter was made 1.75 million years ago in France from a low wall of piled stones topped with branches and perhaps grass.

Grasses or reeds

Mammoth tusk

Skins and bones

People later made more permanent homes from many different materials, depending on where they were and what was available. Some still used wood, stones, and grasses or reeds, but others used a wooden structure of branches covered with animal skins to make something like a tent. Others even made shelters from the bones of animals they had hunted, again covered with skins to prevent the wind from whistling through the gaps. The remains of some bone shelters include the huge tusks and vast bones of mammoths and other large animals that lived alongside and were hunted by humans.

RECYCLED

Some shelters have been found that used bones from animals that died hundreds or even thousands of years apart. This suggests the bones were reused, handed down, or perhaps found.

Animal skins

MOVING ON

Although our first human ancestors evolved in Africa, people are now spread all around the world, living on every continent. Our path to these countries was long and slow.

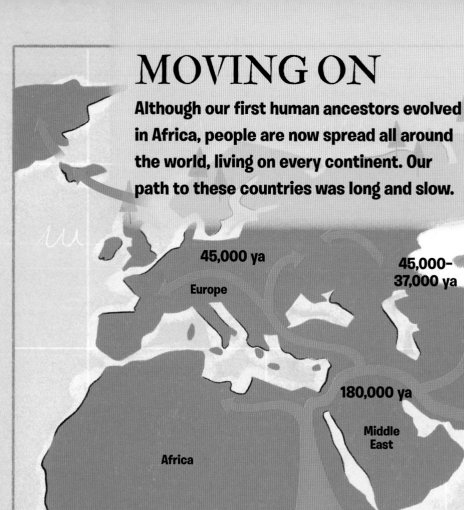

Mammoth hunt, Arctic Siberia

45,000 ya

Europe

45,000–37,000 ya

25,000 ya

Asia

180,000 ya

Middle East

Africa

77,000–120,000 ya

Indian Ocean

1,500 ya

Out of Africa (again)

Modern humans, *Homo sapiens*, emerged in Africa. The first to leave moved out around 180,000 years ago, going first north and east into Asia. Some then turned south toward Indonesia, eventually taking boats across the Pacific to Australia and perhaps the Americas. Others looped north through China and Russia and crossed to North America. Around 45,000 years ago, *Homo sapiens* arrived in Europe from the Middle East or Russia.

Not alone

Our ancestors were often moving into areas where other types of humans already lived, such as Denisovans in Russia and *Homo heidelbergensis* and Neanderthals in Europe. There were also many other types of animals, including "megafauna"—very large animals, like mammoths and giant bears. Today, megafauna are found mostly in Africa, where elephants, hippos, rhinos, and giraffes are still larger than other land mammals. Megafauna seem to have died out in different areas as *Homo sapiens* moved in, perhaps because they hunted them and destroyed their habitats. Climate change probably also played a part in their extinction. In Africa, humans evolved alongside megafauna, so the animals perhaps had time to adapt.

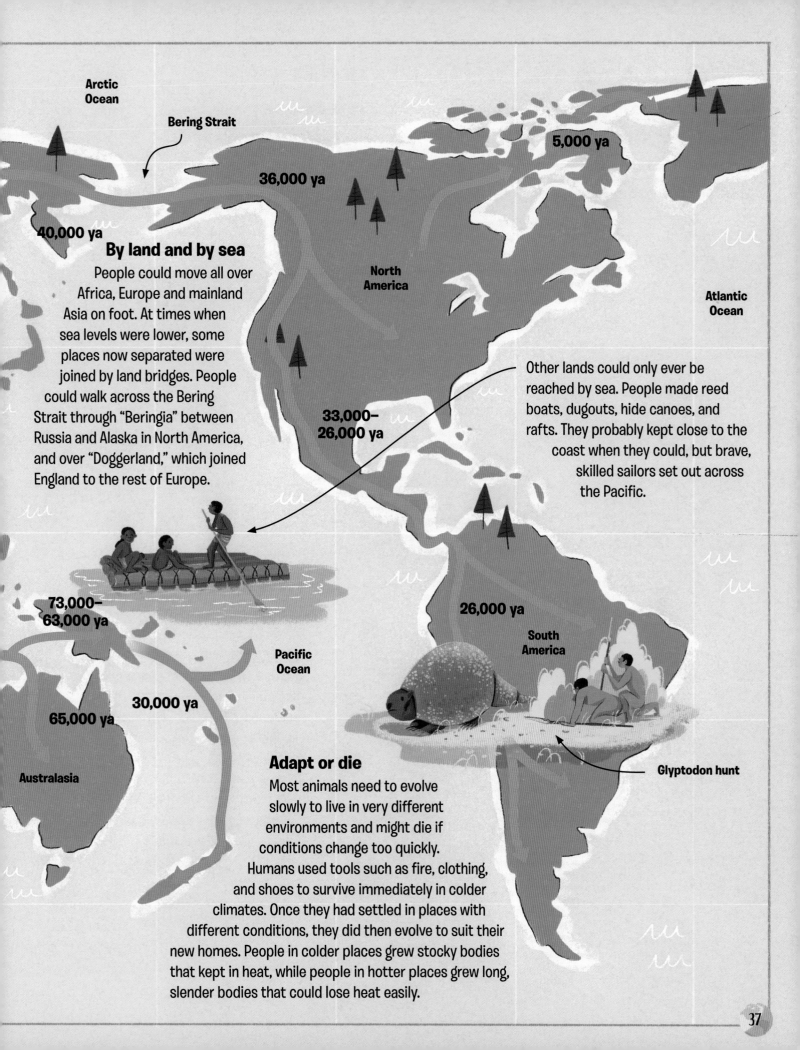

Arctic Ocean

Bering Strait

36,000 ya

5,000 ya

40,000 ya

North America

Atlantic Ocean

By land and by sea

People could move all over Africa, Europe and mainland Asia on foot. At times when sea levels were lower, some places now separated were joined by land bridges. People could walk across the Bering Strait through "Beringia" between Russia and Alaska in North America, and over "Doggerland," which joined England to the rest of Europe.

33,000–26,000 ya

Other lands could only ever be reached by sea. People made reed boats, dugouts, hide canoes, and rafts. They probably kept close to the coast when they could, but brave, skilled sailors set out across the Pacific.

73,000–63,000 ya

26,000 ya

South America

Pacific Ocean

30,000 ya

65,000 ya

Australasia

Adapt or die

Most animals need to evolve slowly to live in very different environments and might die if conditions change too quickly. Humans used tools such as fire, clothing, and shoes to survive immediately in colder climates. Once they had settled in places with different conditions, they did then evolve to suit their new homes. People in colder places grew stocky bodies that kept in heat, while people in hotter places grew long, slender bodies that could lose heat easily.

Glyptodon hunt

WORDS AND PICTURES

Although many other animals communicate, only humans have very complex languages, or make art. With language and art, we can maintain complex social structures, pass on information from one generation to another, talk about abstract ideas, decorate our homes and objects, and make up stories.

First words

We don't know when humans began to develop complex languages, or which species of human first used language. We do know that the shape of the human mouth, teeth, throat, and larynx (voice box) give us a wider range of sounds than other animals can make. The first humans that were physically capable of making the speech sounds were *Homo heidelbergensis*. Some experts think that language began with them. Others believe it is a more recent development, perhaps starting around 100,000 years ago.

Is a picture worth a thousand words?

Spoken language isn't the only way we communicate with other people. While an early human could talk to someone present who understood their language, art can communicate across time. A picture on a cave wall or a carving can be seen and understood by someone the artist has never met, perhaps even long after the artist is dead, by someone who doesn't speak the same language. We can still learn from cave art today—through it, people long dead have told us about their lives and environment. Some cave paintings are so accurate that they have helped scientists discover details of the animals alive at the time. These artists were careful observers of their world. Australian cave art made 12,000 years ago shows ornately decorated people with headdresses, skirts, and bags, giving details of lives we would not have known otherwise, since the objects shown have rotted away.

Early artists

The earliest art doesn't show people or animals, but handprints and pattens. Cave art in Spain 66,700 years old was probably created by Neanderthals, so not only *Homo sapiens* made art.

Neanderthal art in Spain, 65,000 years old, ochre

Dwarf buffalo in Indonesian cave art, 44,000 years old

The oldest known picture of a hunting scene is in Indonesia and is 44,000 years old—it was painted more than 30,000 years before people began to farm the land! Beads and decorated slabs of ocher (sometimes spelled ochre) 70,000 years old have been found in Africa, and people collected pretty crystals 100,000 years ago. A love of beautiful things is not new.

Gwion Gwion rock art in Australia, 12,000ya

SINGING AND DANCING

People probably also communicated by ritual, dance, and music, but these leave few traces. The oldest surviving musical instrument is a flute at least 35,000 years old.

LIFE IN THE DEEP FREEZE

Earth's climate has changed many times over billions of years. It has been much hotter than now, as it was in the time of the dinosaurs, and much colder, as it was during the Snowball Earth events. Scientists distinguish between times when there is ice at the north and south poles and times when there is none. There is currently polar ice, though it's melting. Humans evolved during one of Earth's colder periods (with ice caps), and it is all our species has ever known.

Early humans in Europe adapted to deal with very cold weather during the last ice age.

Hot and cold

The current cold period started 2.6 million years ago, just as our ancestors were becoming human. There have been colder (glacial) and warmer (interglacial) periods within this. We're currently in a warmer period. Over the last half million years, the glacial periods have lasted 60,000–100,000 years and the warmer periods 2,000–25,000 years. The present warm period began 12,000 years ago, ending an "ice age" that started 115,000 years ago. The ice age was at its coldest around 25,000 years ago, when *Homo sapiens* were already the only surviving humans.

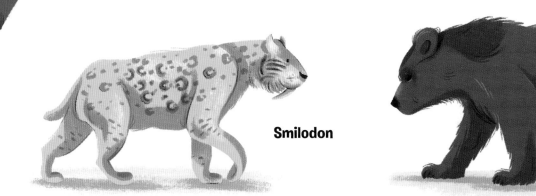
Smilodon

Cave bear

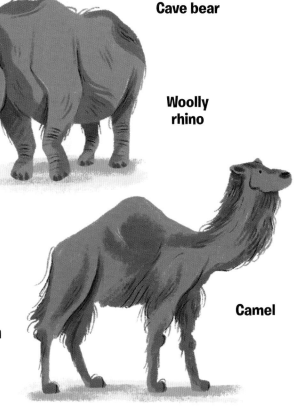
Woolly rhino

Camel

On thick ice

For some of the last ice age and previous cold periods, parts of northern Europe, Asia, Canada, and the northern United States were under an ice sheet up to 1.5 km (1 mile) thick. Humans left northern Europe, including Britain, during each icy period until the last. By the last ice age, humans had adapted well enough to hunt the large animals that lived on the frozen land, including woolly mammoths and woolly rhinos. Cave art shows these and different types of deer and other animals. People could live in the cold because they had fire, they made clothes and shoes from animal skins, and they ate a nutritious diet rich in meat.

Just as importantly, they had language and secure social structures. They could share knowledge and pass it on to new generations, including all they had learned about weather and climate, prey animals and predators, and how to make clothes and shelters. They could cooperate in a hunt for large animals and in sharing and processing the meat, hide, and bones from a kill.

HOW DO WE KNOW?

Cave art often shows the animals living in a region and sometimes shows people hunting them. This gives us clues as to how our ancestors lived alongside animals.

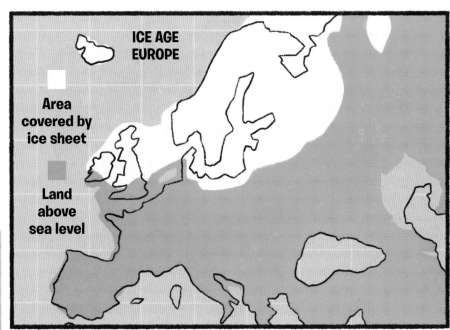

ICE AGE EUROPE

Area covered by ice sheet

Land above sea level

In the last ice age, large areas of Europe were frozen, and some areas now under the sea were solid land, joining Britain and Ireland to the rest of Europe.

Revolution or not?

Some experts think that a revolution in human development at some time between 50,000 and 100,000 years ago produced the skills that make us who we are. They suggest that these extra skills might have made it easy for people to move to new lands–or they might have developed them outside Africa in response to a new environment. People might have changed in Africa, perhaps a long time before our ancestors left the continent.

BECOMING MODERN

How did modern humans become modern? It's not clear whether changes to our bodies, brains, and lifestyles were quick or slow. Whichever it was, the change was complete by about 50,000 years ago.

Homo sapiens

Neanderthals

Survival

Leaving Africa, our ancestors moved into places already occupied by other human species. These others slowly died out. Perhaps the newcomers took too much land or food. Maybe disease or climate change killed them off. In Europe, Neanderthals lived alongside early modern humans for at least 8,000 years, so perhaps their decline had nothing to do with our ancestors.

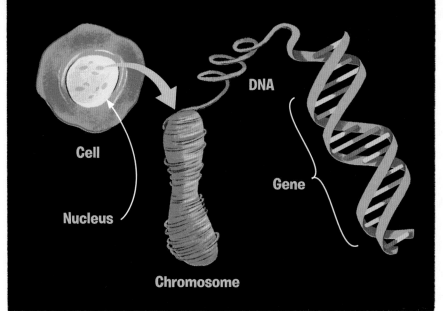

Cell

Nucleus

DNA

Gene

Chromosome

The Neanderthal within us

The "recipe" for you as an individual is stored on your chromosomes in nearly every cell of your body. Chromosomes are made of DNA, a very long, stringy molecule made of two strands twisted together. They carry instructions for building the body of an organism, whether it's you or a carrot. Your DNA makes you a human, and some gives you particular, individual features, such as curly hair or brown eyes. You share most of your DNA with other humans and even more with your immediate family. Lots of genes just tell bodies how to grow and function, no matter what organism they are, so we also share a lot of DNA with completely different organisms, such as tigers, fish, and even plants.

We can collect DNA from the bones of Neanderthals and Denisovans and compare it with our own. Modern people still have some DNA that comes from other human species, showing that there were once families of mixed types of humans.

80%

Cows

70%

Slugs

How much of our DNA do we share with others?

98.8%

Chimpanzees

45%

Cabbages

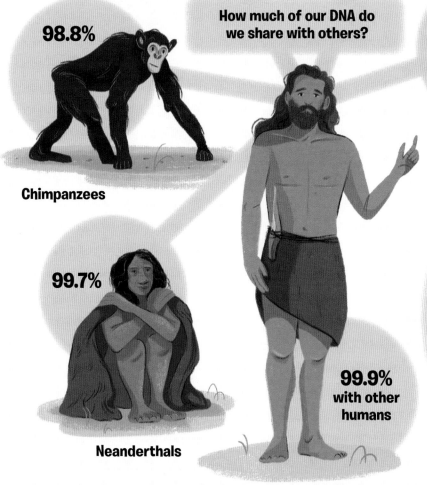

99.7%

Neanderthals

99.9%
with other humans

HOW DO WE KNOW?

Scientists can look at the DNA from any living organism and compare the patterns in it to find similarities and differences. They can also take DNA from bones, skin, and hair of extinct types of human and compare those with modern humans. People with European heritage often have some Neanderthal DNA, while people with Asian heritage typically have more Denisovan DNA.

HERE WE ARE

By 12,000 years ago, the ice of the last glacial period was melting. The Neanderthals and Denisovans had all died out, though we don't know why they died. Early modern humans were left alone, scattered all around the world—only a few islands and the frozen lands of Antarctica and the far north remained uninhabited. With their large brains, skills in language, toolmaking, art, and ritual, they had come through the challenge of living in the ice. Now, the end of the long cold period brought another time of great change, one of the most significant in our history.

Warm enough for wheat

As the climate changed, the plants that grew naturally in different parts of the world also changed. In an area called the "Fertile Crescent," which is in what is now Iraq, Israel, Lebanon, Jordan, Syria, and Egypt, wheat and barley began to grow 14,000 years ago. A group of people called the Natufians in Syria gathered these as they grew wild and used them to make flour, which they baked into a type of bread. They also used the barley to brew beer. They hunted gazelles and other animals that roamed the plains. The Natufians didn't need to move far, since the fertile land and warm weather provided what they needed in a small area. By 12,000 years ago, they had a settled community.

Natufian settlements had tents made of mud, sticks, and animal hides.

Best friends

Even before people lived in settled communities, they had found a companion among the wild animals. Humans first domesticated dogs more than 20,000 years ago. Dogs are descended from wolves, which were probably first hunting companions. The wolves would enjoy a steady supply of food from the partnership, and humans would have help from them in tracking animals. Some wolves might have guarded or rounded up some of the herds that humans hunted from, and they could have protected family groups at night, raising the alarm if dangerous animals or strangers approached.

People probably bred from the animals that suited them best, because they were good hunters, or affectionate, or perhaps good at rounding up animals. As wolves became dogs, the ways in which they behave has changed, as have their bodies. Humans began to have an impact on how other species developed. That influence extended to other animals and to plants in the next chapter of the human story.

Eurasian wolf

Gradually, people changed from following flocks of animals to keeping them nearby.

BUILDING A WORLD

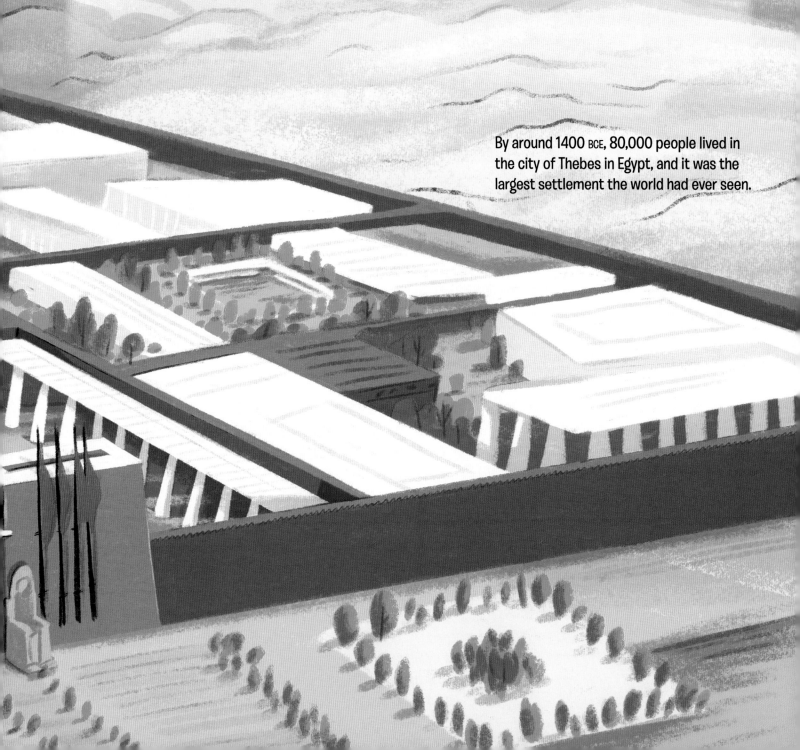

Once people began to settle rather than follow the seasonal patterns of plants and migrating animals, it was a small step to farming, and then building ever larger communities. The start of farming—known as the Neolithic Revolution—changed humankind and its path into the future. To farm successfully, people had to stay in one place, building shelters that were more than just temporary stopping places. This happened again and again in different places around the world. It started 11,500 years ago (9500 BCE), when people began to keep animals and grow crops on the land between Turkey and Israel. Within a few thousand years, settlements became towns and then cities.

By around 1400 BCE, 80,000 people lived in the city of Thebes in Egypt, and it was the largest settlement the world had ever seen.

FOUNDING THE FARM

People began farming first in the Middle East, China, and South America. The way people farmed matched their needs and what was easy to grow where they lived. Where food was plentiful, or there were no animals or crops to domesticate, farming didn't emerge.

Peas:
c.9500 BCE
The eight Neolithic founder crops—emmer wheat, einkorn wheat, hulled barley, peas, lentils, bitter vetch, chickpeas, and flax—were cultivated in the Levant.

FERTILE CRESCENT
11,000 BCE

Auroch (became cattle)
8,500 BCE
Turkey/India

CHINA
9,000 BCE

Camel
3000–1000 BCE
Middle East

Moufflon (became sheep)
11,000 BCE
Mesopotamia

7,000 BCE
Mehrgarh, Indus Valley (Pakistan)

6,000 BCE
France

SUB-SAHARAN AFRICA
5,000–4,000 BCE

Taro, c.8,000 BCE
Southeast Asia

Sorghum (grain)
3000 BCE
Sahel region of Africa

In Mesopotamia, people began domesticating pigs, goats, and wild sheep.

In China and Nepal, people domesticated water buffalo and yak.

POOR FOOD

The diet of early farmers was probably less nutritious than the diet of hunter-gatherers. They ate a less varied diet, based on a small number of farmed crops and animals. Skeletons from thousands of years ago show that people became shorter as farming became established.

Animals at large

People began to keep and domesticate animals before farming crops. They probably started by managing the wild herds that they hunted from, realizing that it was best to kill older and male animals. This left the young to grow up and the females to produce young, which made sure they had animals to hunt in the future. They used dogs to protect natural groups of deer, cattle, and goats from other predators. By choosing which animals to keep for breeding, people began to change and domesticate them, reinforcing useful characteristics.

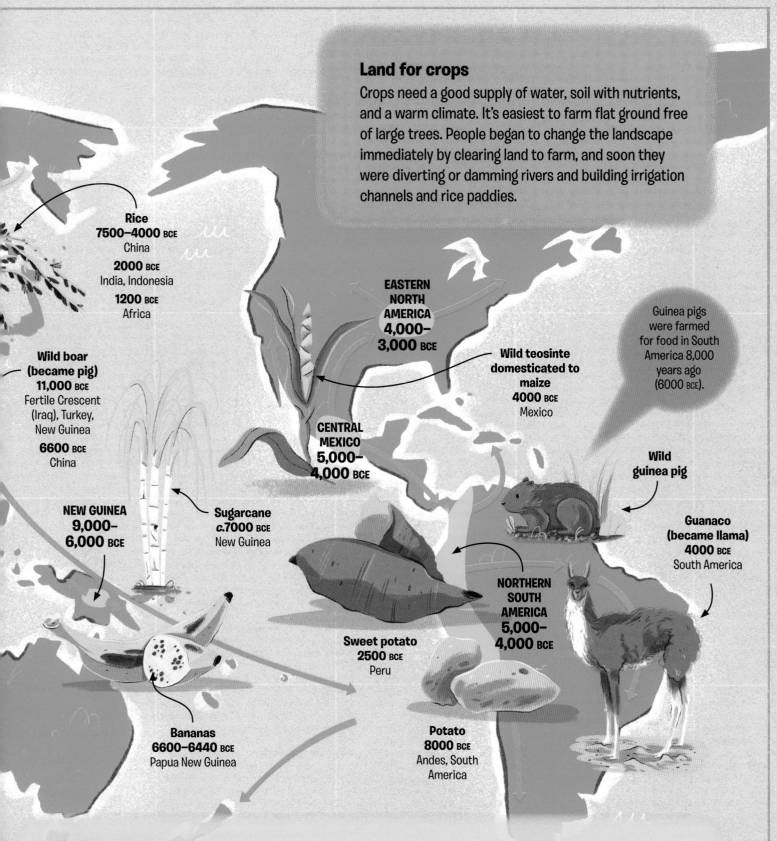

Land for crops

Crops need a good supply of water, soil with nutrients, and a warm climate. It's easiest to farm flat ground free of large trees. People began to change the landscape immediately by clearing land to farm, and soon they were diverting or damming rivers and building irrigation channels and rice paddies.

Rice
7500–4000 BCE
China
2000 BCE
India, Indonesia
1200 BCE
Africa

Wild boar
(became pig)
11,000 BCE
Fertile Crescent (Iraq), Turkey, New Guinea
6600 BCE
China

NEW GUINEA
9,000–
6,000 BCE

Sugarcane
c.7000 BCE
New Guinea

EASTERN
NORTH
AMERICA
4,000–
3,000 BCE

Wild teosinte domesticated to maize
4000 BCE
Mexico

Guinea pigs were farmed for food in South America 8,000 years ago (6000 BCE).

CENTRAL
MEXICO
5,000–
4,000 BCE

Wild guinea pig

Guanaco
(became llama)
4000 BCE
South America

Sweet potato
2500 BCE
Peru

NORTHERN
SOUTH
AMERICA
5,000–
4,000 BCE

Bananas
6600–6440 BCE
Papua New Guinea

Potato
8000 BCE
Andes, South America

For better and worse

Farming produced more food than hunter-gathering, so populations grew. Settlements grew into towns and cities with communal places to store food, trade, celebrate, and worship. But living in larger groups and close to their animals also brought problems. Diseases jumped between species, so that, for the first time, humans caught flu, measles, smallpox, and other diseases that existed before only in animals. Bacteria and viruses changed to live in human bodies and became truly human infections. Most of them still trouble us today.

LIVING TOGETHER

As settlements grew larger, some became cities. The very first small city was probably Çatalhöyük, now in Turkey, about 9,000 years ago. It was home to around 8,000 people. The city grew up on two mounds on both sides of a gully, though the two halves seem to have been occupied at different times.

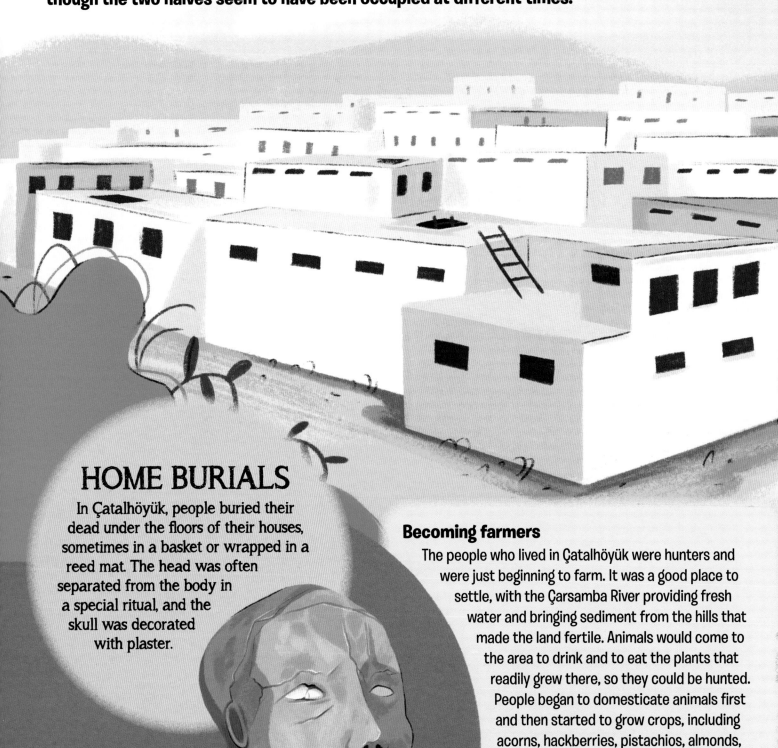

HOME BURIALS

In Çatalhöyük, people buried their dead under the floors of their houses, sometimes in a basket or wrapped in a reed mat. The head was often separated from the body in a special ritual, and the skull was decorated with plaster.

Becoming farmers

The people who lived in Çatalhöyük were hunters and were just beginning to farm. It was a good place to settle, with the Çarsamba River providing fresh water and bringing sediment from the hills that made the land fertile. Animals would come to the area to drink and to eat the plants that readily grew there, so they could be hunted. People began to domesticate animals first and then started to grow crops, including acorns, hackberries, pistachios, almonds, and plums; pulses such as peas, chickpeas, bitter vetch, and lentils; cereals such as barley and wheat; and flax to make linen.

Life on the roof

There were no communal buildings, only homes. People went into their rectangular houses through a hole in the roof, climbing down a ladder or stairs to get in. Only a few had doors in the sides. Most daytime activity probably took place on the roofs, which also served as streets. The houses were closely packed, built right next to each other like the cells of a honeycomb.

The houses were built of mudbrick, plastered and whitewashed on the inside. They were kept very clean, and archeologists have found waste only outside the city. Most homes had a main room and one or two smaller storerooms connected by a very low doorway, only 75 cm (2.5 ft) tall. Ladders, a platform, cooking hearths, and ovens were always on the south side of the main room. All houses were very similar, suggesting that people had roughly equal wealth.

Early artists

The people of Çatalhöyük decorated their houses with wall paintings of geometric designs, human figures, and animals. These decorations were refreshed frequently, sometimes as often as each month. They also kept small clay figures and the skulls and horns of animals, which had been plastered and sometimes decorated with a red pigment.

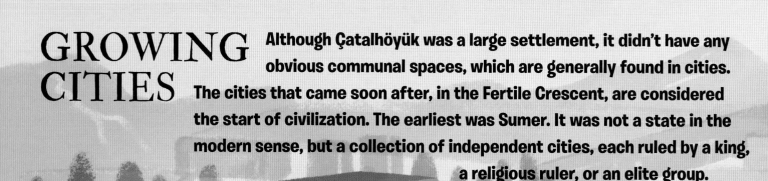

GROWING CITIES

Although Çatalhöyük was a large settlement, it didn't have any obvious communal spaces, which are generally found in cities. The cities that came soon after, in the Fertile Crescent, are considered the start of civilization. The earliest was Sumer. It was not a state in the modern sense, but a collection of independent cities, each ruled by a king, a religious ruler, or an elite group.

A fertile crescent

The Middle East was wetter 7,000 years ago than it is now. Warm sun, combined with plentiful water and fertile soil, made farming easy and productive. The first civilizations grew up in Mesopotamia and Egypt. Mesopotamia lay between two rivers called the Tigris and Euphrates, and Egypt lay along the Nile River. The land around these rivers was regularly flooded by water carrying rich sediment that fertilized the fields. With successful farming, the population grew quickly, and people didn't need to spend all their time finding food. There was time for other work— and spare time led to civilization.

Black Sea

Euphrates

Tigris

Mesopotamia

Mediterranean Sea

Sumer

Egypt

THE FERTILE CRESCENT

Uruk

Nile

Red Sea

Sumerian art

First citizens

Uruk, in Sumer, was probably the first true city. It was about 250 km (155 mi) from the modern city of Baghdad, in Iraq. By 2900 BCE, Uruk was the largest city in the world, covering 4 square km (1.5 square mi). It began as a farming community, with small, individual fields that were kept lightly flooded. When climate change altered the flow of water around 4000 BCE, the people of Uruk changed to a new way of farming, using irrigation channels cut through larger fields. People needed to cooperate to make this work—they could no longer each focus on their individual plot of land. Once it was working, though, it produced around five times as much food. The extra food had to be stored and managed, so the Urukians built places to store it and started systems for keeping and sharing it out. This was the start of civic administration.

Away from the fields

For the first time in human history, many people were freed from spending their time seeking food. They began to specialize in different tasks, sharing work in the community. Some people became expert at making clothes or pots, others at farming or building. There was time, too, for art and culture. From Mesopotamia, we have the first known story—the epic of the hero Gilgamesh—and stunning carvings that show us how people lived.

Gilgamesh

WORDS AND NUMBERS

With language, people can share ideas and pass on knowledge. But with only spoken language, communication is limited. We can only remember a certain amount, and although people amass a lot of useful knowledge in their lifetime, it is lost when they die. The next great step in developing the modern world was writing—a way to make a lasting record of words and numbers.

Sumerian clay tablet

Bone stylus

Reed stylus

Egyptian hieroglyphs

Chinese oracle bone scripts

Cursive, used on ceramics

Angular, carved into bone

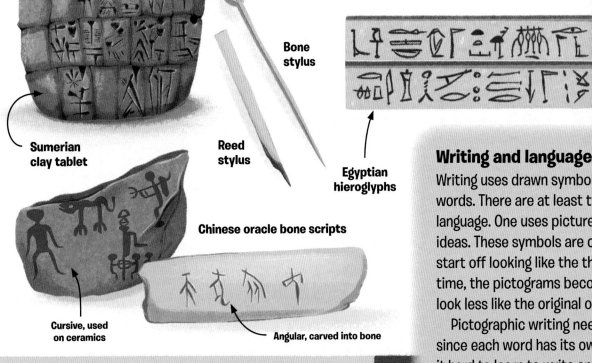

Bird

Horse

How pictograms change to become less recognizable over time.

1500 BCE   **213 BCE**   **after 200 CE**

Mayan scribe & glyphs

Writing and language

Writing uses drawn symbols to stand for spoken words. There are at least two types of written language. One uses pictures to show things or ideas. These symbols are called pictograms and start off looking like the thing they represent. Over time, the pictograms become more stylized and look less like the original object.

Pictographic writing needs a lot of symbols, since each word has its own symbol. That makes it hard to learn to write and read. Many later languages use a smaller set of symbols that represent the sounds of speech. Languages such as English, Russian, and Greek use this system, with alphabets of a small number of letters. What a word looks like doesn't tell you its meaning, but if you can read the alphabet you can pronounce it reasonably well.

The Sumerians began to write with pictograms around 3300 BCE. Sumerian scribes pressed symbols into a soft, clay tablet with a small stick called a stylus using a type of writing known as cuneiform. Baking the clay tablets preserved them—and many still survive 5,000 years later. Pictographic writing developed independently in China and South America, too.

Quipu

Numbers

The first recorded numbers are simple tallying sticks and marks on bones or stones. The Ishango bone from the Democratic Republic of Congo is at least 20,000 years old. Tallying doesn't require counting, since people just make a mark for each item they record—they don't need names for the numbers.

Proper number systems and the start of mathematical thinking followed when cities grew and people needed to keep track of food, other supplies, and taxes. In Mesopotamia and China, people used styluses and brushes to record numbers and words, but in South America numbers (and possibly words) were recorded using a system of knotted strings called "quipu." This system still hasn't been fully deciphered.

A scribe in Mesopotamia writes with stylus and tablet.

55

POTS AND PANS

When people first began to farm, they used tools made of wood, bone, and stone, but within a few thousand years they created metal tools. Metal tools made hunting and farming easier and more productive. The consistent use of metal tools marks the start of the "Bronze Age." It began at different times around the world, but it is usually said to have started first in Sumer around 3300 BCE.

Copper smelting, Mesopotamia

Gold nugget

Beaten and bruised

Metals are found in two forms in nature. Some can exist alone, such as lumps of gold in streams. Others can exist in ores, where they are bound into rock. To extract metal from ore, the rock must be heated, so that the metal melts and separates (smelting). People first used metals that can be used immediately. Gold, silver, and copper can all be found and can be worked "cold"—they're soft enough to be shaped by beating without melting them (though heating makes it easier). Copper was probably first worked in Çatalhöyük about 7500 BCE and in Jarmo, Mesopotamia. Gold, too, was shaped by beating. Too soft to be useful for weapons or tools, gold was only used decoratively.

Hot and bothered

The first mixed metal, or "alloy," used was bronze. Made by melting copper and mixing in tin, it's stronger than copper alone. The molten metal was poured into a shape pressed into sand or clay, and allowed to cool and harden. Copper has a high melting point. Before people could make bronze, they had to discover how to fire clay pottery, because pottery kilns reached temperatures high enough (over 900°C/1650°F) to melt copper.

IRON FROM SPACE

Iron doesn't occur on its own and melts at too high a temperature for early metalworkers to remove it from ore. Yet there are a few early iron objects. They were made by hammering iron meteorites that fell from space. A dagger in the tomb of the Egyptian pharaoh Tutankhamun was made from meteoric iron.

Hot pots

Pottery is made from clay, a type of mineral-rich mud that hardens in heat. People made clay statues at least 12,000 years ago, and clay pots 10,000 years ago in Syria and Turkey, leaving the clay to harden in the sun. Two inventions revolutionized pottery-making: the potter's wheel and the kiln. The potter's wheel, used in Mesopotamia by 3000 BCE, turned a lump of clay so that a potter could make pots quickly and accurately. The kiln was a very hot oven used to "fire" clay, making it much harder. These kilns made bronze-working possible.

Halaf bowl, Syria, 5600–5000 BCE

Tutankhamun's iron dagger with its decorative gold sheath.

57

CIVIC LIFE

A city doesn't run itself. With large numbers of people living in a settlement, it must be well organized to make sure that everything runs smoothly and people have what they need. Civic life, in the form of government, finance, laws, sharing resources, and allotting work tasks, appeared as cities grew.

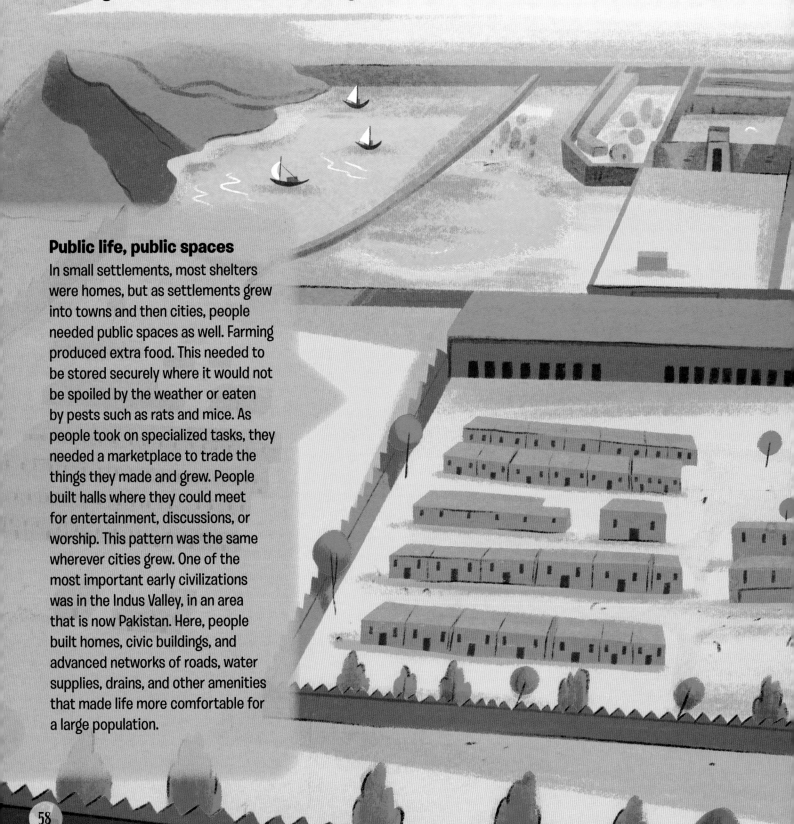

Public life, public spaces

In small settlements, most shelters were homes, but as settlements grew into towns and then cities, people needed public spaces as well. Farming produced extra food. This needed to be stored securely where it would not be spoiled by the weather or eaten by pests such as rats and mice. As people took on specialized tasks, they needed a marketplace to trade the things they made and grew. People built halls where they could meet for entertainment, discussions, or worship. This pattern was the same wherever cities grew. One of the most important early civilizations was in the Indus Valley, in an area that is now Pakistan. Here, people built homes, civic buildings, and advanced networks of roads, water supplies, drains, and other amenities that made life more comfortable for a large population.

Laws

A large number of people living together need rules to guide them and protect the weakest members. The earliest surviving legal code, or set of laws, is the laws of Hammurabi, written around 1750 BCE. Some laws look quite brutal to modern eyes, such as death for burgling a house. Others are considered fair even now—for example, if a builder makes a house badly and a wall falls down, the builder must repair it at his own cost. The rule of law, then as now, was intended to help people live together peacefully and cooperatively.

The Law Code Stele of King Hammurabi

Friends and enemies

As large cities grew up, there were eventually arguments and then battles and wars between them. Cities and later nations began to train soldiers and keep armies, so that they could defend their buildings and surrounding farmland against others. Some used their armies to invade and seize the lands of nearby cities. In this way, some cities grew to govern more and more people, eventually developing into large empires that spread over much land. Empires grew in Egypt, Mesopotamia, the Indus Valley, and China. By 200 BCE, the Qin empire of China ruled over 40 million people—when the world population was only 150-230 million people.

LET'S TRADE

In hunter-gatherer communities, each family caught or found their own food and made their own tools and clothes. In settlements, people specialized—one person might look after goats while another made pots. People would swap with others to get items they didn't make themselves.

Swap?

A straight exchange could be difficult—if you caught a bird but wanted a pot, you would need to find someone who made pots and wanted a bird. Some jobs didn't produce swappable objects —a priest looking after a temple couldn't swap their work for a loaf of bread. People began to trade with tokens instead of swapping objects. A token might have genuine value, like a sack of wheat, or symbolic value, like a type of shell. Tokens with symbolic value became money. People would swap, say, a fish they had caught for a valuable shell. They could then swap the shell for a basket of fruit. They no longer needed to find someone who both wanted what they had and had what they wanted.

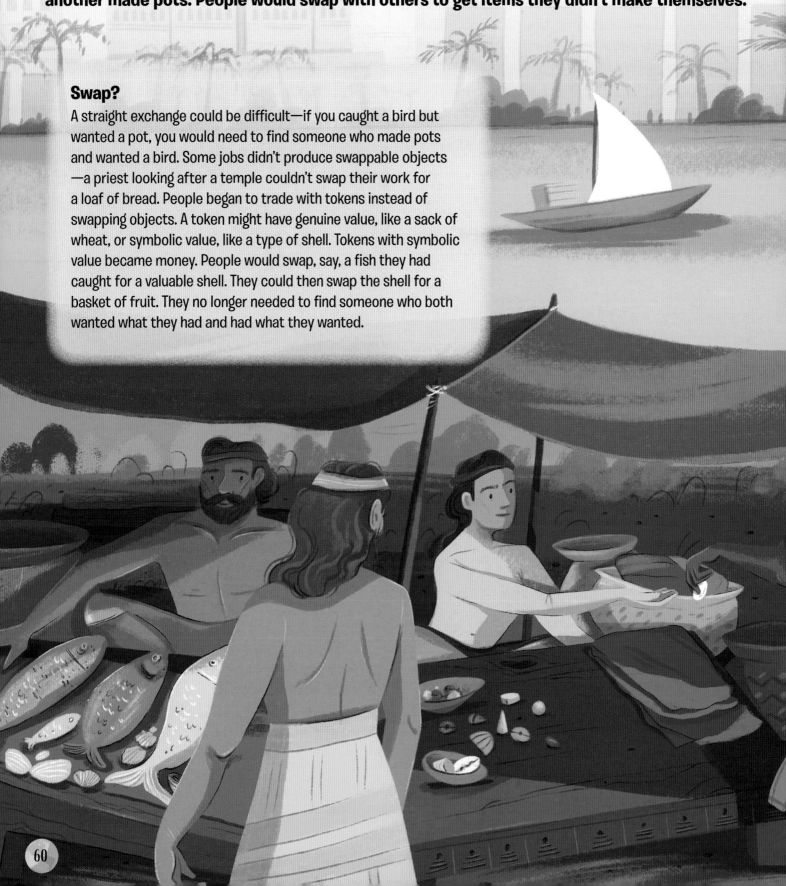

Trade and taxes

A city needs people to work in jobs that benefit the whole community, such as repairing roads or tending the gods. Work like this is paid for from taxes—each person pays some of their income to the city. Taxes were first collected in types of food that could be stored, such as grain, and later in money.

From cows to coins

The best trading tokens are small, portable, and don't rot. A shell or a coin is easier to carry than a cow and doesn't decay like fruit. Tokens can come in different values, too. Swapping a cow for tokens meant that its value could be broken down and spent over several occasions. The first coin, the Mesopotamian shekel, appeared about 4,500 years ago.

Clay tokens representing objects such as cows or quantities of grain were first used in Mesopotamia 5,500 years ago. The tokens were sealed in a clay envelope. The envelope could be broken open later to prove ownership. As people scratched copies of the tokens onto the envelope, showing what was inside, the symbols came to stand for the objects and numbers. The first written records relate to taxes, accounting, and ownership of property.

Clay tokens, Middle East, 5500 BCE

Chinese shell money, 1000 BCE

In China, copies of knives and spades—knife money and spade money—circulated 2,000 years ago. These tokens, up to 20 cm (8 in) long, had only symbolic value.

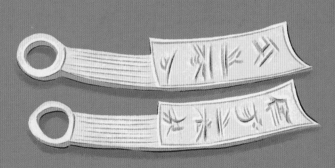

GIANT MONEY

On Yap, a Pacific island, huge "rai stones" were used as money. They were too large to move, so people just agreed that ownership had changed. The name of the new owner was added to the spoken history of the stone.

Rai stone

EXPLAINING THE WORLD

We don't know when people started taking a curious interest in the world around them, looking for explanations of what they saw. Before they could write down their thoughts, stories, and prayers, they made art and special objects, but these can be hard to interpret.

Egyptian creation myth—Nun lifts the boat of the Sun god Ra into the sky.

Sumerian votive figures

Mysteries

Life's mysteries were first explained with stories about gods and spirits. Many cultures have made up stories to answer such questions as how the world began, where the Sun goes at night, what happens to people after death, and what causes terrible events such as earthquakes. Early societies might have tried to please their gods with offerings, celebrations, and worship, asking for help with difficulties, or thanking them when things went well. Small carvings called votive figures suggest that people were doing this in Sumer nearly 5,000 years ago.

Looking at the stars

Prehistoric people tracked the movement of the planets, Sun, Moon, and stars and learned how to predict some of them. We know this because they built structures that line up with the stars or Sun and made objects that show the positions of the stars.

The **Nebra sky disk**, 3,600 years old, shows the Sun, Moon, and a group of stars called the Pleiades, evidence of careful observation of the sky.

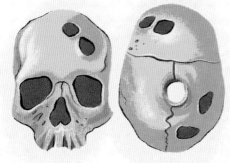

Getting better

People have tried to treat injuries and illness for thousands of years, beginning with splinting broken bones, pulling out painful teeth, and covering wounds. But collections of skulls with holes in show that a more intrusive treatment was common. Drilling through the skull, called "trephining" or "trepanning," was probably used to release evil spirits or cure headaches or seizures. It was performed around the world, using stone drills or scrapers. Many drilled skulls show signs of healing, so the patients recovered—and some even went back for a second or third operation!

People would have noticed the effects of different plants on their bodies, from poisoning to treating illnesses and causing visions. This knowledge about the properties of plants was eventually written down. Medical texts from Egypt nearly 4,000 years ago list medical conditions and their treatments, including medicines and surgical procedures.

Tracking time

Tracking the Sun over a year helped people to plan when to plant seeds and when to expect the seasonal movement of animals and changes in the weather. Calendars could also help people to time religious ceremonies.

Standing in the middle of **Stonehenge**, in England, at midwinter 4,500 years ago, the Sun would have set exactly between the last two upright stones.

CRADLES OF CIVILIZATION

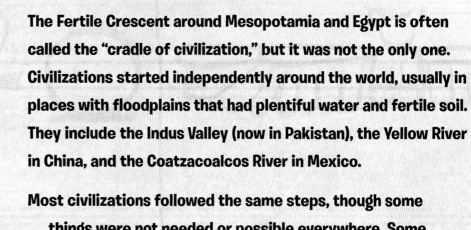

The Fertile Crescent around Mesopotamia and Egypt is often called the "cradle of civilization," but it was not the only one. Civilizations started independently around the world, usually in places with floodplains that had plentiful water and fertile soil. They include the Indus Valley (now in Pakistan), the Yellow River in China, and the Coatzacoalcos River in Mexico.

Most civilizations followed the same steps, though some things were not needed or possible everywhere. Some places had more resources than others, and citizens had different needs. People who lived where there was no clay made no pottery, for example. We know the least about cultures that didn't have writing. Their history, passed on by word of mouth, has often been lost when their civilizations died out or scattered.

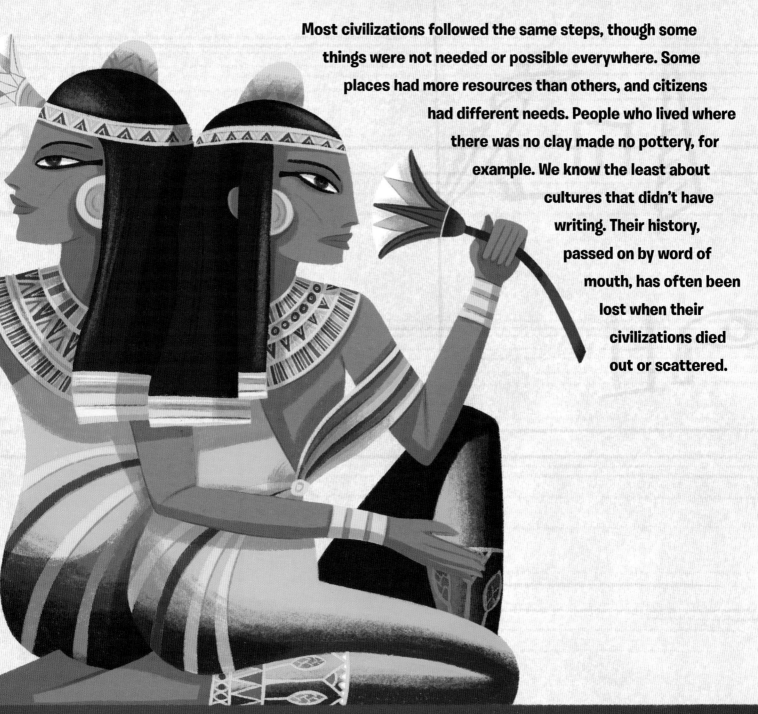

ANCIENT EGYPT

The Egyptians settled along the banks of the Nile River around 7,000 years ago. The annual flooding of the Nile over the land made the soil fertile and the vegetation lush, while the river also provided fish. The Egyptians first formed two kingdoms around 3400 BCE, but they were combined 300 years later beginning the first dynasty of the pharaohs. We know a great deal about the Egyptian civilization because their writing system of hieroglyphs has been deciphered. They left a lot of written records and art recording their everyday lives, their history, achievements, and their myths and legends.

Ancient Egyptians didn't only mummify humans, but also animals they linked with gods, including cats, crocodiles, and ibises.

Top to bottom

Egyptian society was very hierarchical—it had an all-powerful pharoah as ruler, and priests and court officials who were also very powerful. At the bottom of the social structure were many enslaved people. Although we know a lot about what people of higher rank did and how they lived, most individuals' lives were probably very harsh, and we know little about them. Society relied on hard work. The pharaohs had huge pyramids built as their tombs, made by slaves who dragged massive blocks of stone across the desert. But they were built following careful plans that show a good command of geometry and physics.

Life in death

Many documents made on papyrus survive, and the walls of pyramids and other structures are often decorated with pictures and hieroglyphic text. These give details of history, life, and religious beliefs. The Egyptians' religious rites and stories were rich and complex, explaining mysteries such as how the world came about and the place of humans in it. They looked after their dead, packing tombs with offerings for the gods and objects for the dead person to use in the afterlife, including food, furniture, and household objects, as well as buildings such as houses and bakeries.

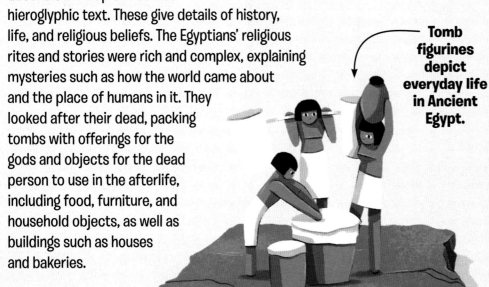

Tomb figurines depict everyday life in Ancient Egypt.

Starting science

The Egyptians built on Sumerian astronomy, learned about the human body, and left the first medical texts. The ritual for dealing with high-ranking dead people involved removing and preserving internal organs and embalming and wrapping the body as a mummy. The mummification process relied on a knowledge of chemicals and anatomy. The precise building of the pyramids, the system of taxes, and measuring of land that was flooded each year all needed a good understanding of mathematics. This emerging knowledge was not lost with the Egyptians but fed into civilizations that came after, in Greece, Syria, and Rome.

Mummification

Ancient Egyptians mummified important people when they died. Parts of the body were preserved in special coptic jars, and the body was put into a decorated coffin.

Coptic jars

The success of the civilization depended on trade, so weights and measures were important.

INDUS VALLEY

The Indus Valley civilization was as great as those of the Fertile Crescent, but we know less about it. Its written language had at least 400 pictograms that were pressed into clay with a stylus, but it hasn't been interpreted. Some developments known from Mesopotamia or Egypt might have appeared first in the Indus Valley.

At its height, the Indus civilization covered an area larger than Egypt and Mesopotamia put together. The cities of Harappa and Mohenjo-Daro were built from around 3000 BCE along the banks of the Indus where the soil was fertile. Life was peaceful and stayed much the same for hundreds of years.

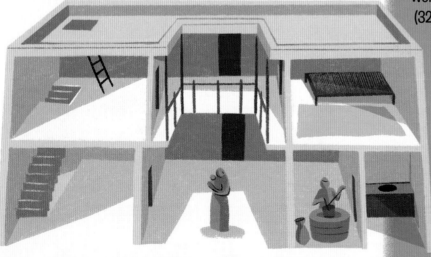

Some houses were built around a central courtyard.

High rise

The cities of the Indus were the first planned cities in the world. Instead of growing slowly from small settlements like the cities of Mesopotamia, they were built on a regular grid. A main street (10 m (32 ft) wide) ran down the middle of each city, with side streets branching from it, all exactly half or two-thirds the width of the main street. Lanes half that width came off the streets. The streets and their drainage gutters were built first and the mud-brick buildings filled in along them. New buildings were often put on top of old ones, so that in some places the city ruins are 7 m (23 ft) deep.

No large temples, tombs, or statues have been found, but a deep pool was probably used for religious ceremonies. Hinduism probably started with the Indus civilization.

A nice life

The Indus Valley seems to have been a peaceful place. Archeologists have found no evidence of war or weapons, and houses were built to a high standard with good drainage, flush toilets, and even a kind of air conditioning. Houses had flat roofs that provided an extra living space, and some had courtyards. Archeologists have found many toys—small figures of people, animals, and objects—and also fine unglazed pottery, and jewelry made of gold, silver, shells, and crystal. People of the Indus Valley possibly invented dice and chess.

Clay seals

Toy cart

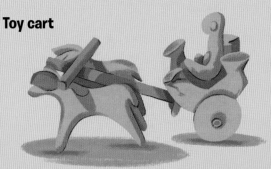

All good things come to an end

All the world's early civilizations collapsed. For the Indus Valley, the end came between 1900 and 1700 BCE. The cities seem to have become overcrowded and not properly maintained, possibly because of climate change, overpopulation, or the end of trade with Egypt and Mesopotamia. Elsewhere, civilizations fell to invaders, war, famine, disease, or changing environmental conditions.

ANCIENT AMERICA

Humans went to America from Asia, arriving in Alaska at least 36,000 years ago. They spread over the vast continent of North America, living in small groups as hunter-gatherers.

City of Tenochtitlán

Parallel paths

The ancient civilizations of the Americas grew up alone, cut off from the rest of the world. Although the first Americans had left Asia long before the start of farming, they took most of the same steps as their left-behind cousins, differing mostly in details. The great civilizations of South America, such as the Olmec, Inca, and Maya, developed complex social structures, and advanced farming techniques and technologies that suited their environments.

Differences began early. Instead of flint, people in South America made blades from obsidian, a black volcanic glass that breaks into naturally sharp shards, making a tool in seconds. Metals were hard to find and extract, and they were used mostly for decorative and ceremonial objects. Although gold was used from 2100 BCE, copper smelting didn't begin until 900–700 BCE. The mountains and rainforest needed different farming methods from the fertile valleys of Mesopotamia and the Indus Valley. Terraces solved the problem of cultivating on a slope. Wheels were of little use in a forested, mountainous land with no animals that could pull a cart, and wheels were used only on toys.

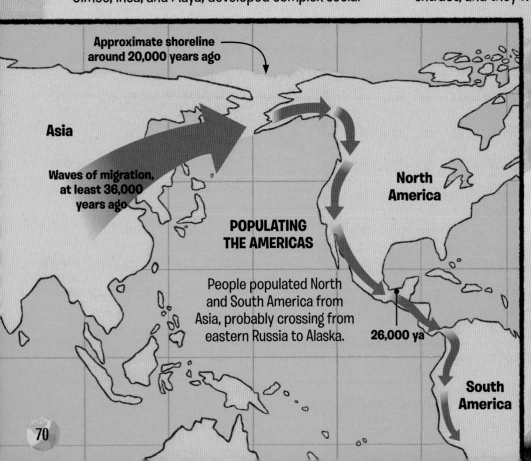

Approximate shoreline around 20,000 years ago

Asia

Waves of migration, at least 36,000 years ago

North America

POPULATING THE AMERICAS

People populated North and South America from Asia, probably crossing from eastern Russia to Alaska.

26,000 ya

South America

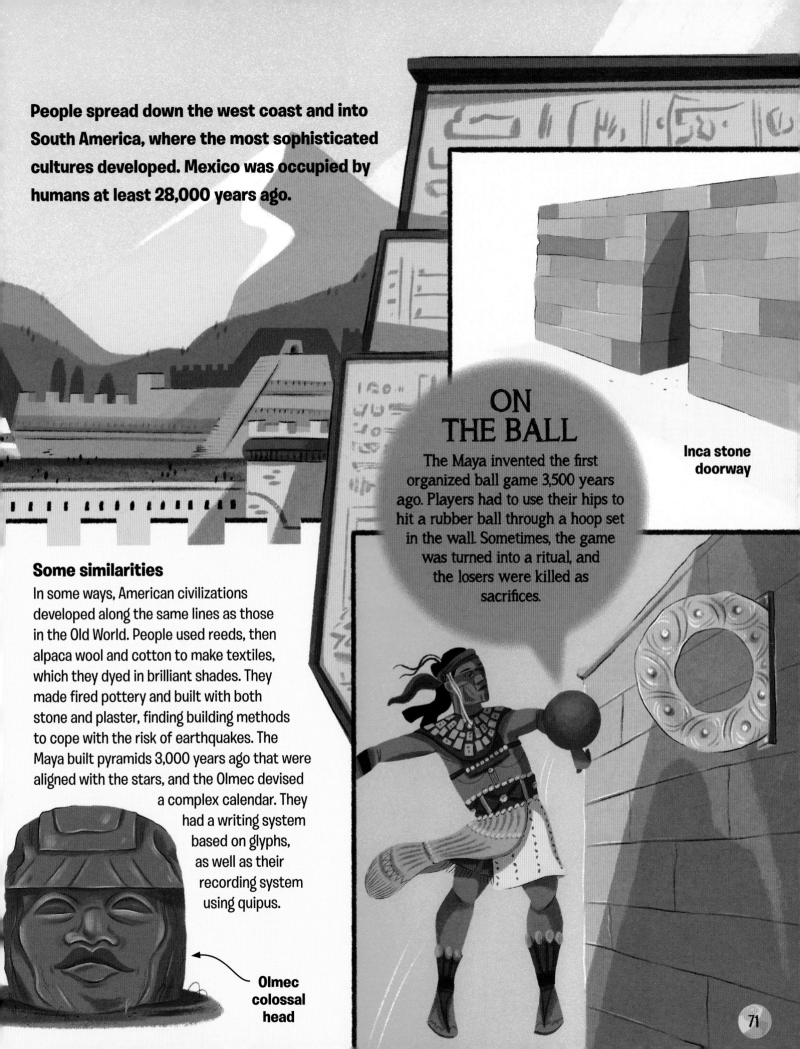

People spread down the west coast and into South America, where the most sophisticated cultures developed. Mexico was occupied by humans at least 28,000 years ago.

Inca stone doorway

ON THE BALL

The Maya invented the first organized ball game 3,500 years ago. Players had to use their hips to hit a rubber ball through a hoop set in the wall. Sometimes, the game was turned into a ritual, and the losers were killed as sacrifices.

Some similarities

In some ways, American civilizations developed along the same lines as those in the Old World. People used reeds, then alpaca wool and cotton to make textiles, which they dyed in brilliant shades. They made fired pottery and built with both stone and plaster, finding building methods to cope with the risk of earthquakes. The Maya built pyramids 3,000 years ago that were aligned with the stars, and the Olmec devised a complex calendar. They had a writing system based on glyphs, as well as their recording system using quipus.

Olmec colossal head

IT'S ALL GREEK

The first great Bronze Age civilization grew up on the Greek island of Crete. The Minoans' success was built on trade, which they carried out by sea using fleets of advanced ships. They had two early written languages that have not been deciphered. What we know of them comes from later writings and from the beautiful art they left showing their lives.

Palace at Knossos

Model of a Minoan house

Trading empire

The Minoan civilization grew through trade. Using large boats with both oars and sails to cross the Mediterranean, they traded with mainland Greece, Cyprus, Syria, Anatolia (in Turkey), Egypt, Mesopotamia, and Spain. They traded essential foods and materials including ceramics, copper, gold, silver, and tin, and also luxuries—olives, figs, wine, and saffron.

A land of palaces

Crete is a long, narrow island with a lot of coastline. Early settlements on Crete were small villages and farms where people farmed their own food and made the pots and textiles they needed. Soon, larger settlements grew along the coast, and people began trading with other islands and the Greek mainland. These grew into societies grouped around palaces. The capital was Knossos, with three other major palaces elsewhere on the island. Although we call them "palaces," this is a modern term. They might not have housed kings and queens at all—we don't know how Minoan society was organized. They certainly had large areas that were used for storage, and spaces for plenty of people to sleep. They might also have been used for rituals, entertainment, workshops for craft activities, and even as law courts. They were decorated with impressive wall paintings and other art.

Minoan fresco (wall painting)

The island of Santorini as it is now, its middle blasted away by a volcanic eruption.

Santorini

Mediterranean Sea

Catastrophe!

Some kind of disaster, possibly an earthquake, destroyed the Minoan palaces around 1700 BCE. They were built back bigger, along with many additional smaller palaces, and the civilization thrived again—but not for long. A massive eruption of the volcanic island Santorini around 1600 BCE largely destroyed the Minoan port at Thera. It caused a tsunami that wrecked many settlements around the Greek islands and mainland. By 1450 BCE, the Minoan civilization had collapsed. It's likely that the after-effects of the eruption badly affected farming, causing trade to collapse. Invaders and rebellion within Crete could have made things worse. The Mycenae moved in from mainland Greece to rule Crete, building new palaces and also roads, bridges, and other infrastructure. The Mycenae eventually became the ancient Greeks. Their language and their myths based around many gods fed into this later, great culture.

RISE AND FALL

It's easy to think that once a civilization has developed, it can continue forever. But advanced civilizations—such as Minoan Crete—are surprisingly fragile. They rely on their resources, links with other societies for trade, and the climate and environment to which they are suited. Changes to any of these can be disastrous.

The city of Troy fell in the twelfth century BCE.

The late Bronze Age collapse

Around 1250–1150 BCE, something terrible and unexplained happened in the eastern Mediterranean. The late Bronze Age civilizations came to a sudden and violent end; nearly every large city was destroyed or abandoned. Some were never occupied again, and some devastated areas took more than a thousand years to recover.

Many factors probably came together to cause the collapse. They may have included natural disasters, political unrest leading to rebellions, disrupted trade networks, and invasions. We know that there were earthquakes and that climate change caused drought and famine during this period.

TROUBLE IN TROY

The sacking of the city of Troy is one example of the type of catastrophe that faced many cities from the twelfth century BCE onward. According to the Greek poet Homer, the Greek army laid siege to the city and smuggled their soldiers through the walls inside a wooden horse presented as a gift. It sounds unlikely!

After the fall

The Bronze Age was followed by the Iron Age. This began at different times around the world as people learned how to melt iron ore, extract the iron, and strengthen it into steel by adding carbon. It began first in Turkey around 1200 BCE.

Iron and steel weapons were stronger than those made of bronze. A large army of foot soldiers armed with iron swords and spears could easily overcome a traditional smaller army that relied on war chariots and bronze weapons.

An iron sword

Sea People

Hittite state

Assyria

Mycenean Greece

Egypt

From the sea

Ancient Egyptian writers recorded that unidentified "Sea People" attacked Egypt and other civilizations from the thirteenth century BCE. Coming from the Black Sea and northern Mediterranean, they might have been pirates, invaders, migrants, refugees, or a mix of all four. These mysterious newcomers possibly played a part in ending some of Earth's first great civilizations.

EMPIRE IN THE EAST

Early farming communities started 8,000 years ago along the banks of the Yellow and Yangtze Rivers in China. From these, towns and cities grew up to form one of Earth's greatest civilizations. China is bordered by desert to the north and mountains to the west. Its civilization developed in isolation with no early contact with others.

Oracle bones and irrigation

We know little about the earliest times in China, as written records date from only 1250 BCE. They are on oracle bones—small scraps of shell and bone scratched with early Chinese characters. Some early records report that "Yu the Great," who supposedly lived 2123–2025 BCE, built irrigation channels to carry floodwater from the Yellow River safely into the fields and dredged silted-up riverbeds. This solved the problem of devastating flooding. Whatever Yu's actual role, Chinese civilization flourished in the Bronze Age. Small states combined to become the heart of the later Chinese empire.

Oracle bone

Terracotta warriors

GUARDED AFTER DEATH

When Qin died, he was buried with an army of thousands of terracotta warriors larger than life-size. Many still lie buried under the hills near Xian.

Another collapse

But, as in the Mediterranean, Chinese civilization ran into problems. In the eighth century BCE, local leaders grew in power until eventually China consisted of hundreds of small states, some no larger than a village. At the same time, invaders from the north and changes in technology added to the disruption. Even so, this time, called the Spring and Autumn period, produced some great intellectual work, including the important philosophies of Tao and Confucius.

Great Wall of China

Confucius was a great Chinese philosopher who encouraged people to behave in a moral way with justice and kindness.

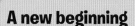

Confucius, around 550-479 BCE

A new beginning

The many small states began to combine, reducing to a final seven large states that fought each other during a time known as the Warring States period, 476–221 BCE. At the end of it, Qin Shi Huang unified China and began an empire that would survive more than 2,000 years, from 221 BCE until 1911.

Qin's dynasty lasted only 15 years, but it was momentous. By reducing the powers of aristocrats and landowners, Qin gained direct control of the peasants, who made up most of the population. He could then make sweeping changes and start large projects. He began connecting patches of wall along the borders, starting the Great Wall of China. He introduced standardized currency, weights and measures, and a single writing system to bring the state together and encourage trade.

A WORLD OF WATER

Most early civilizations grew up where there were good resources for building farms and cities. They were usually near rivers, which provided water, fish, and fertile land. They had enough surrounding land that an expanding population could claim more as it was needed. But the Polynesian people took a different track. They were talented navigators and sailors living on the tiny islands of the Pacific Ocean. Instead of cities with trade, complex social hierarchies, and ever larger buildings, they built simple homes on islands that each supported relatively few people.

There and gone

The Polynesians left no written records of what they accomplished or how they organized their society. But we know they were the best sailors in the world for thousands of years. The islands they lived on were small. As populations grew and they needed more space, groups would set out to find another island to live on. The way they lived on the islands differed, with some having more formal civic structures and others being largely communities of farmers and fishers. They did not rely on metals, and they needed little clothing in the warm climate. But they were just as intelligent and skilled as the people who built great urban civilizations elsewhere.

Shell astronomical map used for navigation.

Polynesian navigators used temporary maps based on the positions of the stars, marked out with shells on the sand.

Boat trips

The Polynesians navigated the open oceans without modern maps or equipment. Instead, they observed the currents in the sea, wind, the stars, and the routes taken by seabirds. They gathered this information and perfected their skills over hundreds of years of seafaring. Navigation by the stars is easier in regions near the equator, since the position of the stars doesn't change much. The Polynesian navigators took advantage of this to sail the Pacific Ocean, which covers one-third of Earth's surface. Their boats, made without metal tools, were fashioned from wood and reeds. They consisted of two parts joined together like a modern catamaran, and had triangular sails and oars.

Island homes

Polynesians made their homes on around 1,000 islands dotted around the vast Pacific Ocean. Originating in Taiwan, an island in the South China Sea, around 3000 BCE, they possibly even reached Antarctica and South America in their canoes. They certainly reached Australia. Over a period of 2,000 years, they sailed between and settled the islands of western Polynesia, making journeys of hundreds of miles in small canoes.

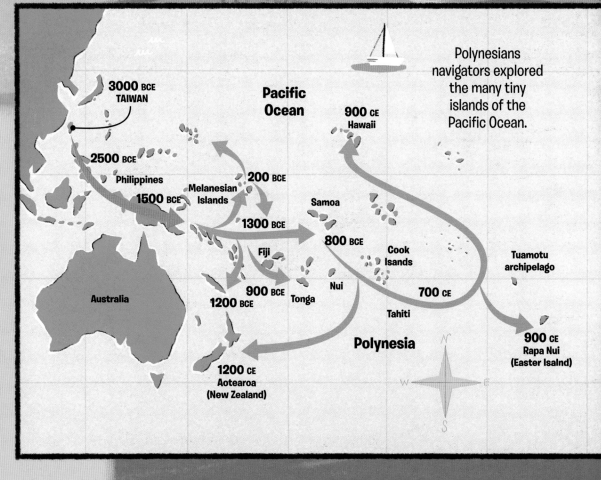

Polynesians navigators explored the many tiny islands of the Pacific Ocean.

3000 BCE TAIWAN
2500 BCE
Philippines
1500 BCE
Melanesian Islands
200 BCE
1300 BCE
800 BCE
Samoa
Fiji
900 BCE
1200 BCE
Tonga
Nui
Cook Isands
700 CE
Tahiti
Tuamotu archipelago
900 CE Hawaii
Pacific Ocean
Polynesia
900 CE Rapa Nui (Easter Isalnd)
Australia
1200 CE Aotearoa (New Zealand)

NOMADIC LIFE

Not every culture has built a civilization. Just as the Polynesian navigators spread out over the islands of an ocean with no central organization, people in some other places also lived without cities. Some moved around overland as nomads or lived in small unconnected groups. Some of these ways of life continue to this day.

On the move

In northern China, Mongolia, and the Russian steppe, groups of nomadic pastoralists have moved in summer with their animals between feeding grounds and hunted in winter for hares and foxes with tamed eagles. This lifestyle still continues after at least 3,000 years.

Hunting with eagles, Mongolia

Life on the ice

The Saqqaq people lived in west Greenland 2400–1300 BCE, with no access to metals and no chance to grow crops. Living in small tents, they hunted ducks, geese, seabirds, caribou, seals, walrus, porpoise, baleen whales, and fish. They made tools from slate, agate, quartzite, rock crystals, and bone and used knives, harpoons, and bows with arrows all made from stone, bone, and antler. They burned driftwood and local trees for fuel, and they heated water in animal skins and wooden containers by dropping in hot stones. People lived throughout the cold northern regions in similar ways. They left no written records, so we know nothing about how they organized their societies. What we know of them comes from the objects they left behind.

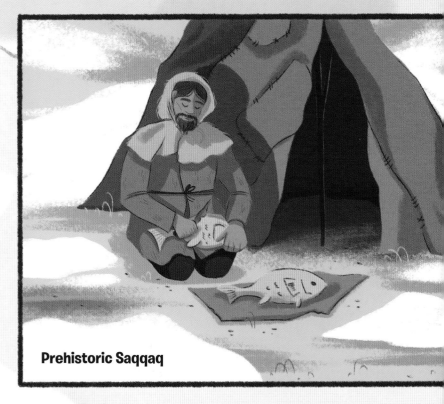

Prehistoric Saqqaq

A world apart

At the other end of the world from the Saqqaq, aboriginal Australians and Torres Strait Islanders also developed a culture that had no metals or writing. Some early Australians lived a fully nomadic life in the dry interior of the land, moving around to find food. Others, nearer the coast, had a seminomadic lifestyle. They moved in a fixed circuit during the year, using the same settlement places for thousands of years. Torres Strait Island communities had permanent settlements.

Aboriginal settlement

Early Australians used wooden throwing sticks, stones, and spears with throwers to kill land animals such as kangaroo, emu, and wombats, and made nets, traps, harpoons, and lines with hooks to catch fish. They also ate snakes, birds, and insects and their larvae. Agriculture increased 3000–1000 BCE, but there were few domesticated animals. Dingos (like wild dogs) were domesticated for hunting, and eels were farmed to eat. The Torres Strait islanders domesticated pigs and cassowaries (large, flightless birds).

THE WORLD COMES TOGETHER

One of the first clashes between civilizations began with the Persian invasion of parts of Greece in 547 BCE. The Greeks won the wars of 499–449 BCE and, more than 100 years later, conquered much of near Asia under Philip of Macedon and Alexander the Great.

Five thousand years ago, the world was occupied by thousands of isolated pockets of humanity. Most knew nothing of each other's existence. Some were on islands, others were cut off from one another by impassable seas, dense forest, deserts, or mountain ranges. Only a few civilizations of the Old World encountered one another. Mesopotamia and Egypt grew up side by side, but they had no contact with China or the Indus Valley, let alone with Mesoamerica or Australia. Even within continents, the land was a mosaic of isolated civilizations.

Between the collapse of the Bronze Age and around 1800 CE, all geographical barriers were overcome. As people began to travel farther, they met more and more others. They traded, fought, exploited one another, and shared stories, resources—and diseases—as they forged a single human world.

THE MODERN WEST STARTS HERE

The Bronze Age collapse left scattered and struggling societies that took centuries to recover. One of the first new civilizations to emerge was in Ancient

Rooted in the past

The Greeks didn't have to invent everything from scratch. Egypt and Mesopotamia survived the Bronze Age collapse better than many places, and some of the intellectual work done there—in mathematics, for example—was taken up by the Greeks.

Starting the modern world

The Greeks introduced new ideas in philosophy, politics, science, art, and literature. Their language is fully understood, and we have many records of what they thought and how they lived. The Greeks produced plays in large, purpose-built, open-air arenas, some of which are still performed today. They left poems and legends that have inspired other artists for 2,500 years. From 508 BCE, they even had the first democracy—a political system in which people vote for their lawmakers and decision-makers (though women and slaves could not vote in Ancient Greece).

Greece. Modern-day Greece has a chunk of European mainland and a large number of small islands. Ancient Greece was a collection of separate societies on the mainland and islands, many with different languages. Over hundreds of years, these grew into city-states with a single language and writing system. Much of western culture has grown from Ancient Greece.

Athens had the first democratic government, with free men of the city voting for people to govern them.

New patterns of thought

The Ancient Greeks included the first "modern" western thinkers. Thales of Miletust is sometimes called the first scientist because he set out to find natural explanations for events.

Instead of accepting that gods cause things like earthquakes or illness to happen, he looked for causes in the physical world. For him, the movements of the stars and planets should be explained in terms of science. For earlier thinkers from the Middle East to China, they had seen astronomical events as omens—an eclipse might mean a change of ruler, for example.

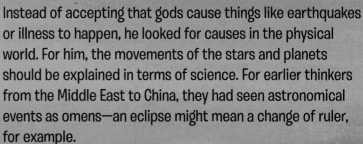

FROM GREECE TO ROME

When Alexander the Great conquered the city-states in 338 BCE (see page 88), he spread Greek culture far and wide rather than destroying it. The Greek city-states finally fell to an invasion by the Romans in 146 BCE. Again, instead of crushing Greek civilization, the Romans adopted much of it and spread it farther around Europe.

FROM EAST TO WEST

Trade was very important in bringing people from different places and cultures together. Although people have traded locally for thousands of years, from around 300 BCE trade networks began to cover much larger distances.

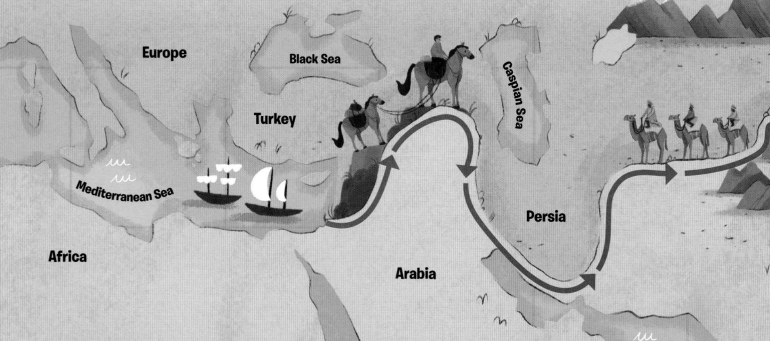

Silk and spice

Trade routes grew to move goods between the east and west after China opened to trade under the Han dynasty in 130 CE. Traders made the long trek from Europe and the Middle East to fetch silk, spices, jewels, and jade. In return, horses, textiles, and glassware flowed into China. The overland route, known as the Silk Road, went from Turkey through Central Asia and across the Gobi desert. This was not a single road but a collection of routes through dangerous lands beset by natural perils and bandits. It was a long way, and covering 6,500 km (4,000 mi) at the pace of a walking horse or camel took a long time. Trading posts and markets along the way grew into wealthy cities.

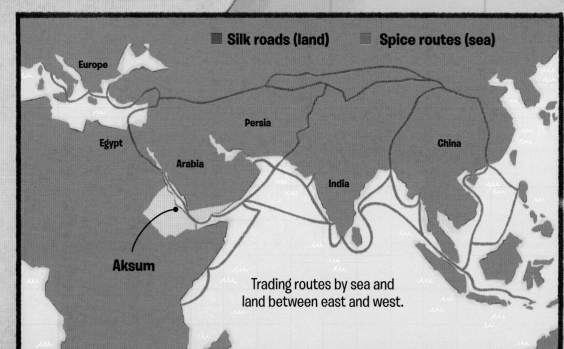

Silk roads (land)   **Spice routes (sea)**

Trading routes by sea and land between east and west.

Getting along

Asia, Europe, and Africa are all connected by land, but there was little communication between distant parts until around 2,000 years ago. Barriers, such as mountains and deserts, and wide, empty stretches of land made travel difficult, dangerous, and often unrewarding.

As civilizations in Europe and the Middle East came into contact with those in India, Africa, China, Japan, and Korea, people learned of and wanted objects available elsewhere. Trade began to open up the world.

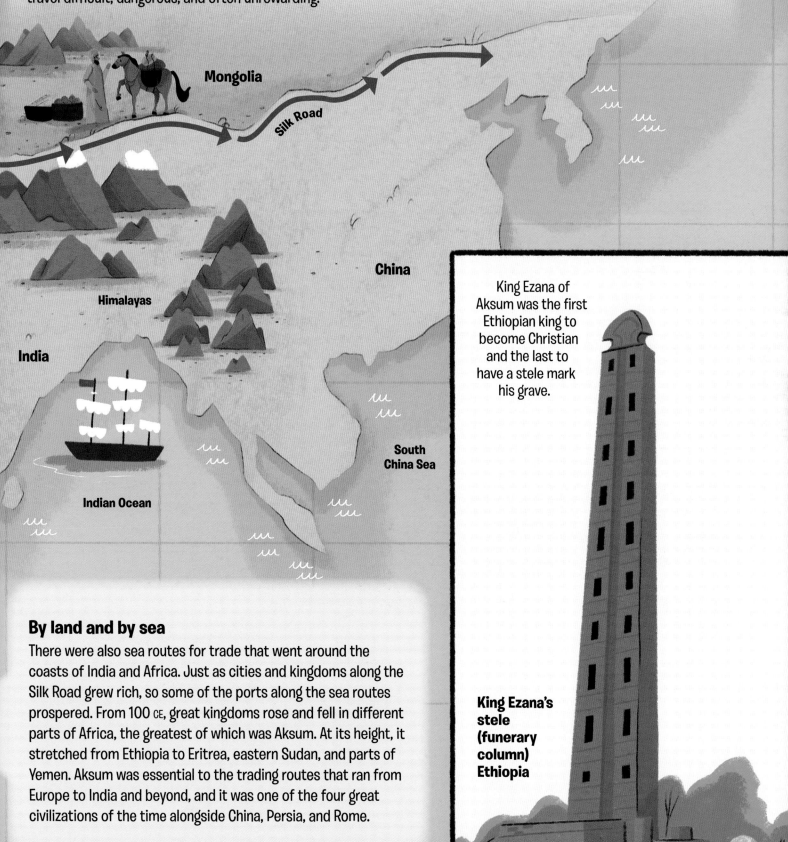

Mongolia

Silk Road

China

Himalayas

India

South China Sea

Indian Ocean

King Ezana of Aksum was the first Ethiopian king to become Christian and the last to have a stele mark his grave.

King Ezana's stele (funerary column) Ethiopia

By land and by sea

There were also sea routes for trade that went around the coasts of India and Africa. Just as cities and kingdoms along the Silk Road grew rich, so some of the ports along the sea routes prospered. From 100 CE, great kingdoms rose and fell in different parts of Africa, the greatest of which was Aksum. At its height, it stretched from Ethiopia to Eritrea, eastern Sudan, and parts of Yemen. Aksum was essential to the trading routes that ran from Europe to India and beyond, and it was one of the four great civilizations of the time alongside China, Persia, and Rome.

ON THE WARPATH

Trade was one way in which cultures engaged with each other; war was another. Around the world, small states grew larger by attacking and taking over places nearby. Ambitious rulers competed to seize areas with valuable resources, getting supplies of food, metals, wood, and enslaved or indentured workers.

From Greece to Pakistan

In Europe, Alexander the Great combined the Greek city-states and conquered an empire that stretched from Greece to northwest India. It was one of the largest empires in early history, covering more than 5 million square km (2 million square mi). The discoveries and developments of many early civilizations were brought together in it. Alexander the Great was never defeated, but he died young in 323 BCE at just 32 years old, and without him his empire broke apart.

Roman aquaduct

When in Rome ...

The Roman empire, centered in Italy, dominated the Mediterranean and North Africa for hundreds of years. The Romans built excellent roads and bridges, which made it easy to move soldiers and resources around quickly. They gave the local people better living conditions and responsible jobs within the empire, so that they were unlikely to rise up against the Romans. The empire eventually first into two parts, east and west, and then in 476 CE, the western part fell to invaders from northern Europe.

From strength to strength

Although the Macedonian and Roman empires were large, the empire of the Mongols, 1,000 years later, was far greater. It became the largest empire the world had ever seen. The ruler Genghis (or Chinghis) Khan first united Mongolia in 1206 and then captured parts of China. His army was known for being brutal, and people terrified of attack often gave up, helping the empire build more quickly. New military techniques and technologies such as gunpowder and the stirrup helped them conquer vast areas of land.

For 100 years, Mongolia was in control of much of the land the Silk Road passed through. The empire

Genghis Khan

stretched from China to Hungary in Europe and was the largest continual tract of land ruled by one person the world has ever seen. At its largest, it covered 24 million square km (9.3 million square mi), more than any empire except the British in the nineteenth and twentieth centuries. In 1242, before invading Austria, the Mongol army turned and returned home. They were possibly driven back by bad weather, which caused famines and turned the plains to marshes.

under the reign of Genghis Khan in 1227
the empire at its greatest extent in 1279

Europe

Mongolia

Persia

China

Arabia

India

The extent of the Mongol empire under the great emperor Genghis Kahn and his heirs.

THE MEDIEVAL MIND

After the death of Alexander the Great, Greek language and Greek scholarship continued in places such as Egypt and Syria and as far away as India. The result was a rich blending of Greek ideas with the discoveries made in older civilizations.

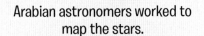

Arabian astronomers worked to map the stars.

Alchemists invented tools and processes still used today.

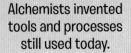

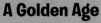

A Golden Age

In the countries of the Middle East, the intellectual work of the Greeks continued without a break, but in Europe it faded from view. People became unable to read the Greek texts and forgot the work of the Greeks. But in the Middle East, Islamic Arabs of the Abbasid Dynasty, starting in 754 CE, continued that work. They built the city of Baghdad (now in Iraq), which attracted scholars as well as traders. From 786 CE, the caliph al-Rashid brought in expert thinkers from as far away as China and India. The "House of Wisdom" became a great library and a focus for learning. Great works in Greek and other languages were translated into Arabic, studied, and expanded by talented Arab scholars.

In Baghdad, Arab scholars not only translated but extended works on medicine, astronomy, mathematics, science, and other subjects. The foundations for the modern intellectual world were laid in the House of Wisdom, drawn from all the major civilizations of Europe, North Africa, and Asia. Learning was very highly valued by the Abbasid caliphs, and intellectual life flourished until invading Mongols destroyed the House of Wisdom in 1258.

Round city of Baghdad

Back to Europe

The learning of the Arab world was brought back to Europe from the eighth century. Texts were translated again, this time from Arabic into Latin. Latin had been the language of the Romans and was used around Europe for important documents. Sharing a single language made it easy for knowledge to spread through Europe.

The Christian Church was at the heart of learning in Europe. Monks copied documents by hand, called manuscripts, and collected them in large libraries. Learning was restricted to the people who could read and who understood Latin. That was mostly men who worked in the Church, the law, or medicine, or who were wealthy, though some wealthy women and nuns could read. Manuscripts were rare and expensive. There was little incentive or opportunity for poorer people to learn to read, and they rarely did.

GODS, FOR GOOD OR ILL

People in all civilizations have developed religions that offer a spiritual framework for life. Religious codes help societies remain stable by setting out what people can do, banning acts such as theft and murder. Many religions include stories or myths that try to explain mysteries, such as how mankind came into being. But religions can also cause conflict within and between cultures.

One god or many?

Religions can have just one god, such as Christianity, Islam, and Judaism, or many gods, such as Hinduism or the religion of the Inca. Buddhism has no gods at all, but is a code for living and a set of spiritual beliefs rooted in the teachings of Buddha. Early religions had many gods and spirits, often with different responsibilities or living in special places such as streams, forests, or rocks. Offerings of food, prayers, and even animal or human sacrifices might be given to gods by people hoping for a successful harvest or hunt.

Ganesha
(Hindu god)

Among the many gods revered in Ancient Egypt, **Osiris** was god of the underworld (above), **Anubis** was the god of death (middle), and **Horus** (right) was the king of gods.

Explaining life

Religions gave people a way of explaining the world's mysteries through stories, answering questions such as what happens after death. In Ancient Egypt, the whole world was said to have been created by the Sun god, Ra. The daily passage of the Sun across the sky was explained as Ra sailing a boat from east to west. Each night, he died and descended to the underworld, only to be reborn the next day and rise again. Stories like this explained events that we now explain with science.

GODS FOR PROGRESS

From the earliest times, religion has spurred the growth of civilizations and cultures. People developed astronomy to create calendars both for farming and religious festivals. They made art, architecture, music, and writing to make things in honor of their gods and to preserve and spread religious teachings.

Reims cathedral, France

Comfort and conflict

Although religions have brought comfort and meaning to people's lives, they have also brought bitter conflicts. People sometimes start cruel and destructive campaigns against people with different beliefs. Religions that demand that their followers convert people with different religions have led to wars. During the Middle Ages, the Christian Church in Europe launched violent "crusades," which waged war against the Muslims in the Middle East to seize places they each considered sacred to their own religion.

CATASTROPHE—BLACK DEATH

The Middle Ages saw the greatest catastrophe that humankind has ever suffered—the Black Death. Plague spread from the East, probably starting in Mongolia, and devastated Asia, North Africa, and Europe. The Americas and Australasia were spared as there was no link between them and the rest of the world.

The disease called the Black Death was bubonic plague, a deadly infection carried by fleas. It caused fever and often buboes—hard, painful swellings that turned black, giving the disease its name. There were three different forms, depending on how people became infected, but all versions killed most people who caught it.

Plague route

The Black Death was carried to Europe and Africa along trading routes by land and sea. It then looped back to India and the Far East. It spread more slowly than the Covid-19 pandemic that started in 2020, since it could travel only at the same speed as people walking, sailing, or riding on horseback.

The Black Death ravaged the world for more than five years. Even when the terrible wave of death had passed, plague remained and cropped up in small and large outbreaks for the next 500 years.

Going backward

Plague killed up to half the population in the countries it struck, but the destruction was uneven. Some towns and villages were completely destroyed, while a few were entirely spared. Apart from the terrible deaths, plague had a huge impact on societies. It brought social breakdown, with not enough people living to farm the land and provide food. Those left living were distressed and shocked. There were neither enough workers nor burial spaces to bury the dead, and bodies were often simply tipped into large pits and covered with earth.

In many places, people assumed they had angered their god and that the plague was a punishment. There was no knowledge of how germs cause diseases and so the remedies people tried ranged from praying to strange medical potions that had no effect. In the places where they separated sick people, the spread of the disease sometimes slowed, but otherwise nothing anyone tried worked.

With few people to farm the land, crops failed and livestock went uncared for.

BUILDING BACK

As societies slowly recovered, there were often changes. Where there were not enough people to work, wages increased. Poor people now had a little more power and money, and they had more say in where they worked and what they did. For some, life was not quite as harsh as it had been.

The spread of the Black Death.

EUROPE

ASIA

AFRICA

THE RISE OF SCIENCE

The change toward the modern world began in fourteenth-century Italy with the Renaissance—a new direction in art and thinking that showed confidence in human abilities. In painting, sculpture, and building, people were inspired by Ancient Greece and Rome. Art celebrated human bodies and achievements. People questioned old ideas and took a new approach.

Read all about it!

A single invention from the mid-fifteenth century revolutionized the spread of knowledge—the first printing press. It printed books using metal letters that could be arranged into pages of text. Suddenly, books could be produced quickly and in large numbers. Knowledge became available to many more people. With more books, more people learned to read and write. The printing press was vital to the explosion of knowledge.

Gutenberg press

Bodies uncovered

People began to investigate the human body through dissection, discovering what lies inside it and thinking again about how it might work. Over the following centuries, they discovered how the blood circulates, how the gut digests food, and the mechanics of how bones and muscles help us to move.

No longer central

In 1543, the Polish astronomer Nicolaus Copernicus argued that the Sun and other planets do not orbit (go around) Earth, but instead the Sun is central. It was an important step in looking beyond holy texts for evidence of how the universe works. It was a long time before the idea was widely accepted.

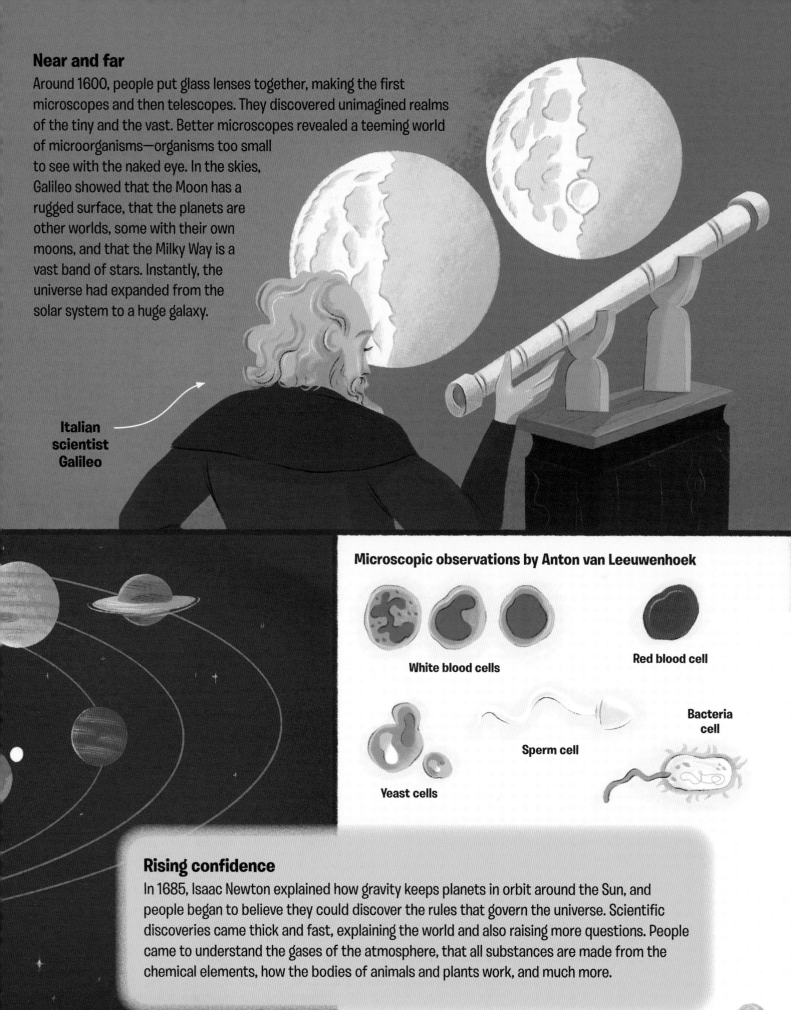

Near and far

Around 1600, people put glass lenses together, making the first microscopes and then telescopes. They discovered unimagined realms of the tiny and the vast. Better microscopes revealed a teeming world of microorganisms—organisms too small to see with the naked eye. In the skies, Galileo showed that the Moon has a rugged surface, that the planets are other worlds, some with their own moons, and that the Milky Way is a vast band of stars. Instantly, the universe had expanded from the solar system to a huge galaxy.

Italian scientist Galileo

Microscopic observations by Anton van Leeuwenhoek

White blood cells

Red blood cell

Yeast cells

Sperm cell

Bacteria cell

Rising confidence

In 1685, Isaac Newton explained how gravity keeps planets in orbit around the Sun, and people began to believe they could discover the rules that govern the universe. Scientific discoveries came thick and fast, explaining the world and also raising more questions. People came to understand the gases of the atmosphere, that all substances are made from the chemical elements, how the bodies of animals and plants work, and much more.

DISCOVERY AND CONQUEST

At the same time as Europeans made great strides in art, science, and technology, they began to explore farther afield, making long journeys by ship. This began in the spirit of exploration, and advancing trade but the impact went far beyond that. It brought together people of widely separated continents who previously knew nothing of each other's existence. It went badly for those in the lands being "discovered" by adventurers from the West.

As the world was known to be spherical, it seemed clear that by sailing west a ship could cross the sea to get to China or India. Europeans had no knowledge of North or South America, the Pacific Ocean, Australasia, or Antarctica.

The world as Europeans saw it in 1490, before they knew of the Americas and Australasia.

The route to India

Hoping to find a direct sea route to India, Cristoforo Colombo set out to cross the Atlantic Ocean in 1492. The first land he reached was the Bahamas, which he believed to be islands near India or China. The West Indies get their name from this mistake. In 1497, John Cabot sailed to North America.

These arrivals spelled disaster for the people already living in these lands. They were slaughtered, enslaved, tortured, abused, and robbed of their land and possessions. Europeans also brought with them diseases that were new to the indigenous Americans—flu, smallpox, and measles killed millions who had no immunity to them. Over the following centuries, people hoping for wealth or a better life, and criminals deported to save the cost of prison, landed in the Americas, destroying societies thousands of years old. People from Portugal, Spain, Britain, Holland, and France became the new Americans.

Lands to the south

Around 100 years later, in 1606, the Dutch sailor Willem Janszoon landed in Australia. There were no serious plans to colonize this land until 1788. Then Britain needed somewhere else to send prisoners and chose Australia. In Australia as in the Americas, white settlers pushed the indigenous people to the margins of their own lands and treated them as inferior, even subhuman. Many were abused well into the twentieth century.

India at last

Soon after Columbus sailed to America, Vasco da Gama sailed around Africa to land in India. Europeans went to India to set up trading posts. In the 1800s, the British and French competed to gain control of India, Britain winning. A similar invasion of Africa happened in the second half of the nineteenth century (see page 106). The world was coming together—but under the rule of white Europeans, not as equals.

Early arrivals traded with local people, but murder and abuse soon followed as Europeans stole the land from its inhabitants.

MAKING OUR WORLD

By 1800, the world was a single, connected place. There were no more vast, inhabited landmasses to be chanced upon by sailors and adventurers. Travel around the now-connected world was becoming easier and easier, with steam-powered ships and trains. The steam engine was first used to drive machines to do tasks previously done by skilled craftspeople. This period, from around

1750 to 1900, is called the Industrial Revolution. It marks the beginning of the modern world, with its mass manufacturing processes, the movement of people into towns and cities, and the start of the pollution and climate change that now threaten our lives. Today, electricity and computers power the devices that make our lives possible, and the world is connected virtually as well as physically.

WORLD OF WORK

Some scientific discoveries were put to work in new technology. The Industrial Revolution began in the late eighteenth century and gathered pace in the nineteenth century. It was a time of rapid change in which many tasks became mechanized (carried out using machinery). Starting in Europe and then North America, industrialization changed how people worked and lived. Changes spread, so that we now live in a connected, industrialized world.

The power of steam

The first useful steam engine was built in 1712. This burned coal to heat water, producing steam that could be used to drive machinery. It was used to pump water out of mines, which often flooded. By the end of the century, improved steam engines powered factories, and in the 1800s they drove trains and ships. The steam engine made the Industrial Revolution possible.

Rise of the machines

Among the first tasks mechanized were spinning and weaving cloth. Soon, work once done by skilled craftspeople was completed more quickly by machines. It was more profitable for the factory owners, but less rewarding for workers. The same happened in other industries. Mechanization changed the landscape and lives. The impact spread beyond the industrialized countries as it led to reduced imports from other countries, impoverishing their populations.

DANGER SIGNS

A growing population that wanted more products from factories threatened the natural world. People hunted some animals almost to extinction, cut down great swathes of forest, and ripped open the land searching for coal and oil. Burning fossil fuels began to change the atmosphere. Land, air, and water became polluted with the waste from factories and transportation.

Whales were killed in large numbers by industrial whaling ships from North America.

From farm to factory

In the early 1700s, most people in Britain, where the Industrial Revolution started, lived in the countryside. They made a living by farming, or from crafts such as making cloth or pottery. By 1850, most people lived in towns and cities, and many goods were made by machines. Coal to fuel the machines was dug from the ground, and the machinery itself was made in huge forges from molten metal. Most jobs in factories, forges, and mines were unpleasant and dangerous; many were done by children. With terrible living conditions and low wages, people lived short lives, working long hours and troubled by illness and injuries from their work. Cities grew larger and dirtier—a pattern repeated around the world in the twentieth century.

Forests were cut down for wood, and to clear land for farming and building.

KINGS, CAPITAL, AND COMMUNISTS

Throughout history, there have been rich and poor people, and often enslaved people below the poor. In the countryside, the poor often had barely enough to live on and might starve if their crops failed. The Industrial Revolution led to a new class of poor people who lived in towns. Eventually, the poor pushed back against systems that were unfair to them.

Old and new ways of living

The earliest societies were often monarchies. A single, powerful ruler such as a chieftain, pharaoh, or king made the laws and ruled with absolute power that often passed down through a family. The ruler was usually supported by an army or by religious leaders who often kept order with brutal punishments.

The Ancient Greeks and Romans both experimented with democracy—a system in which people vote for representatives who set the rules for everyone. But women, slaves, and men without property had no vote. These were brief experiments, but in the 1700s, things began to change. American colonists declared independence from Britain in 1776. White men who owned property could vote for representatives and a president. In France, the rulers and their king lived extravagantly while the people struggled to survive. A revolution overthrew the king and his government. More revolutions happened in Europe in the 1800s. Democracies began to emerge around the world, and later, many of them allowed women to vote. Sometimes, democracies were taken over by dictators. These were rulers who overthrew democracy, taking more power for themselves.

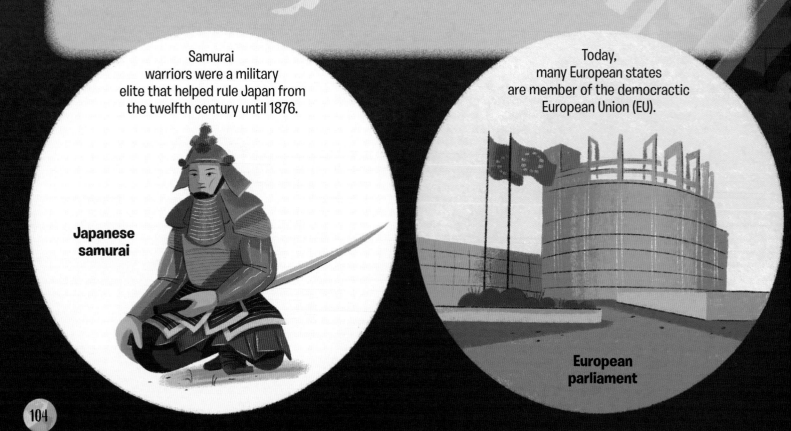

Samurai warriors were a military elite that helped rule Japan from the twelfth century until 1876.

Japanese samurai

Today, many European states are member of the democractic European Union (EU).

European parliament

During the French Revolution, many of the ruling classes were killed using the guillotine.

From one to all

Revolutions in China and Russia in the twentieth century overthrew powerful rulers. After long, troubled times, communist regimes emerged. These intended to remove the difference between rich and poor by having the state own all property on behalf of the people. But people in these countries suffered shortages of food and other essentials, lived with harsh law enforcement, and had no say in how they would be ruled. By the middle of the twentieth century, the world had many different political systems, including traditional monarchies, democracies, communist states, and dictatorships.

In China and Soviet Russia, Communism forced people into an equal but poor living standard that was marked by brutality.

Chinese farm workers

People who spoke against Communism were often punished and imprisoned.

WINNERS AND LOSERS

While factories drew people from the countryside to terrible lives in European towns, an even worse fate struck many other people. As Europeans moved into America and the West Indies, they needed people to work the land, growing food and crops they traded overseas.

Their solution was the worst of all—from the early 1600s, the settlers turned to slavery. Greedy colonists could make more money if instead of paying workers they used enslaved people, who earned no wages.

Africa had many great civilizations with beautiful cities and advanced cultures. There were written languages older than many European languages.

Mosque at Timbuktu, Mali

Lies about slavery

Those involved in the trade in enslaved people tried to excuse their terrible business by claiming that people in Africa were inferior to white people. This was entirely untrue. There is and never has been any evidence that ethnicity is linked with intelligence or skills. Even if these lies had been true, they would not excuse the abuses enslaved people suffered.

Sailing into slavery

People were first captured by African traders who sold them to white traders at the coast. There, they were packed into overcrowded ships and taken across the Atlantic Ocean. It was a long and dangerous journey. They were kept in terrible conditions, and many people died on the way. Once there, enslaved people were treated as property and could be bought and sold. Any children they had were born into slavery and were also owned. Enslaved people were forced to grow rice, tobacco, sugar, coffee, and cotton. This continued until the late nineteenth century. Enslaved African people were finally freed in the USA in 1865, after the American Civil War.

Ravaging Africa

After stealing people, European nations began stealing land in Africa. There was a network of well-established kingdoms and civilizations in Africa that had existed for centuries, but in much of the land it was difficult to move around, and there were also many smaller towns and settlements. The invaders had better weapons, well-organized armies, and could build vast, modern transportation networks in the places they conquered. From 1881 to 1914, European nations carved up Africa between them in the "Scramble for Africa."

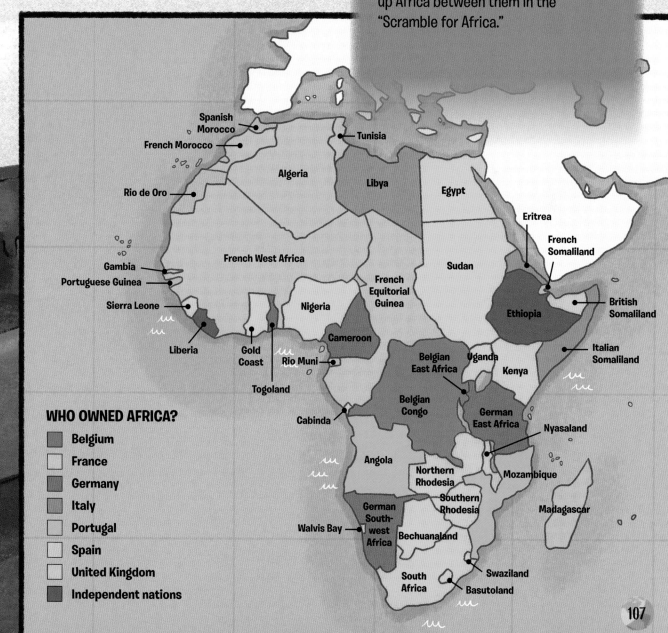

WHO OWNED AFRICA?

- Belgium
- France
- Germany
- Italy
- Portugal
- Spain
- United Kingdom
- Independent nations

Spanish Morocco
French Morocco
Tunisia
Rio de Oro
Algeria
Libya
Egypt
Eritrea
French Somaliland
Gambia
Portuguese Guinea
French West Africa
Sudan
French Equitorial Guinea
British Somaliland
Sierra Leone
Nigeria
Ethiopia
Liberia
Gold Coast
Rio Muni
Cameroon
Belgian East Africa
Uganda
Italian Somaliland
Togoland
Kenya
Belgian Congo
German East Africa
Nyasaland
Cabinda
Angola
Mozambique
Northern Rhodesia
Southern Rhodesia
Madagascar
German South-west Africa
Walvis Bay
Bechuanaland
South Africa
Swaziland
Basutoland

CENTURIES OF SCIENCE

The rise of science that began in the 1600s has continued and gathered pace ever since. In the eighteenth and nineteenth centuries, people discovered more about our world and how it works. In the twentieth century, they began to use knowledge of science to harness new sources of power and to make materials and even organisms never seen in nature. By mastering science, humans changed the world more than ever.

Excavating dinosaur fossils

Down with the dead

As the long history of Earth and life on it became clear, our view of ourselves and our place on Earth changed forever. By 1900, geologists had realized that Earth is billions of years old and was once home to animals and plants that have since died out. The discovery of many types of dinosaur fossils in the nineteenth century and the explanation of evolution challenged prescientific versions of our origins.

Diplodocus

In sickness and in health

From the 1850s, biologists learned how germs cause infection and found ways to protect health. Operations became possible and safe with the use of anesthetics and antiseptics. In the twentieth century, researchers developed antibiotics—medicines that fight infections caused by bacteria—and new treatments for even very serious conditions such as cancer and organ failure. Improvements such as a better diet, clean drinking water, and vaccinations led to people living longer. The world population has risen from under two billion to eight billion in the last 100 years.

By changing the genes (genetic information) of organisms, we can change what the organisms are like.

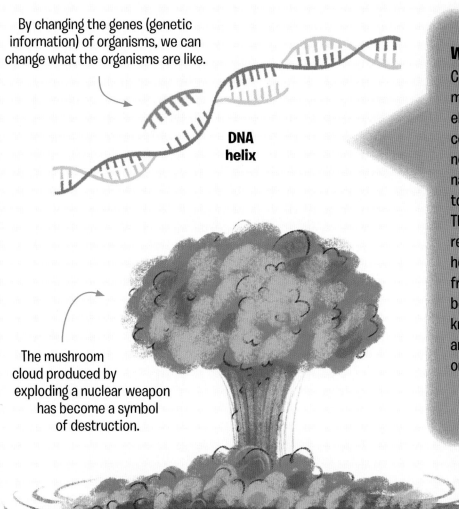

DNA helix

The mushroom cloud produced by exploding a nuclear weapon has become a symbol of destruction.

What we're made of

Chemists learned how everything is made from the atoms of the chemical elements put together in different combinations. They made entirely new, useful materials that don't occur naturally, such as plastics, and pesticides to protect crops from bugs and disease. The energy locked inside atoms was released for nuclear power. Figuring out how living things inherit characteristics from their parents, experts in genetics began to change organisms. This knowledge brought us new medicines and vaccines, crops resistant to disease or drought, and other benefits.

Many people don't get enough exercise to stay healthy.

The dark side

These developments have not been entirely positive. New materials don't break down naturally and can cause problems in the environment. Nuclear power can be used in devastating weapons as well as power plants. Pesticides disrupt the natural balance of the ecosystem. Pollution from our industries floods the skies, soil, and waterways. Though we came to understand the importance of exercise and good diet, we also replaced natural exercise with using cars and replaced healthy, fresh food with highly processed food.

WORLDWIDE DISASTER

Since the late 1700s, trade, and often wars, have kept people around the world in touch constantly, with people, goods, and even diseases passing between them. For some individuals, this has brought profit and success; for others it has brought hardship. The first twenty years of the twentieth century brought two truly global disasters—war and pandemic.

All at war

World War I began in Europe in 1914. A Bosnian Serb killed an Austro-Hungarian archduke in protest at Austro-Hungary ruling Bosnia. This sounds like a very local problem, but the countries of Europe had promised to help each other in the case of war. As a result, more European countries were drawn into the conflict. Those that had built empires dragged more countries into the clash, too. Australians, Indians, Canadians, and soldiers from many African countries became caught up in the war. China and Japan became involved because of their links with Germany and Britain.

"A war to end all wars"

World War I turned into four years of slaughter. The soldiers, particularly those fighting in the muddy trenches of France and Belgium, endured untold horrors. Many died, many suffered terrible, life-changing injuries, and most survivors never recovered mentally and emotionally from the experience. Large areas of land were devastated, with people and countries made poor. Around the world, 8.5 million soldiers and 13 million civilians died. Although people said it would be the war to end all wars, World War II started in 1939.

Pandemic

War was quickly followed by a worldwide pandemic of a particularly deadly strain of flu. It probably began in Kansas, USA, in 1918 and spread to Europe and beyond, carried at first by soldiers moving during and after the war. Over four waves, flu infected a third of the world's population, around 500 million people. Somewhere between 50 and 100 million people died. Most of the people who died in the pandemic were young, previously healthy people. This dealt a devastating blow to economies and families still reeling from the war.

A CENTURY APART

One hundred years after the flu of 1918 ravaged the world, Covid-19 became another worldwide pandemic. Though its toll has been terrible, it's dwarfed by the flu of 1918. To have had the same impact on today's population, Covid-19 would have needed to have killed 265–530 million people worldwide.

The world at war, again

World War I ended with a peace treaty that severely punished the losing side. Resentment and extreme social problems in Germany after the war led to the rise of the dictator Adolf Hitler and his Nazi Party. Hitler began a racist campaign, declaring Germans to be the "master race" and planning to remove people he considered inferior, principally Jewish people. Germany invaded Poland in 1939, starting World War II. Again, countries around the world became involved. Over six years of war more than 70 million people died. The war saw the first use of nuclear weapons, and the Holocaust—the Nazis' slaughter of Jewish people in concentration camps. Other groups killed included disabled people, homosexual people, Black people, Roma, and Poles. Nazi Germany was defeated in 1945 by the Allies: Britain, USA, and the USSR (Soviet Russa).

BEYOND THE WORLD

Humankind is the first species to leave planet Earth and begin to explore space. Humans have been into space and have landed on the Moon, and they have sent spacecraft to other planets in the solar system. Two craft have gone even farther—into interstellar space.

ISS
(International
Space Station)

Stargazing

The stars and planets have fascinated us for thousands of years. With the invention of the telescope in 1608, astronomers began to learn far more, discovering that there are other worlds beyond ours. The twentieth century revealed that there are farther galaxies and that the universe is unimaginably vast. With better telescopes and developments in mathematics and physics, we have come to understand a great deal about how the universe formed and how it works. Our knowledge takes us far beyond this tiny speck of a planet, lodged in one arm of an average-sized galaxy.

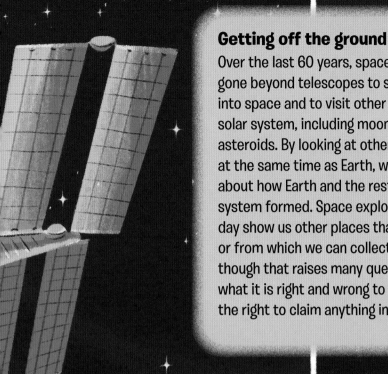

Getting off the ground

Over the last 60 years, space exploration has gone beyond telescopes to sending craft into space and to visit other bodies in the solar system, including moons, planets, and asteroids. By looking at other objects formed at the same time as Earth, we can learn about how Earth and the rest of the solar system formed. Space exploration might one day show us other places that we can live— or from which we can collect resources— though that raises many questions about what it is right and wrong to do, and who has the right to claim anything in or from space.

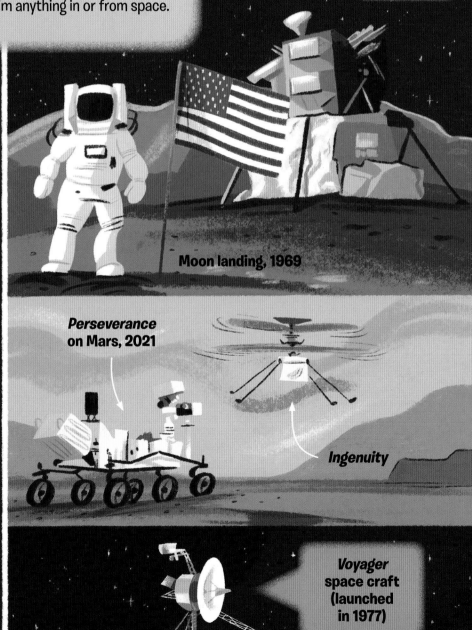

Sputnik 1 (launched in 1957)

Moon landing, 1969

Perseverance on Mars, 2021

Ingenuity

Voyager space craft (launched in 1977)

Are we alone?

One of the most important questions that investigating space might answer is whether Earth is the only place in the universe that has intelligent life—or any life at all. So far, we know of no other life beyond Earth. Astronomers have discovered that there are probably billions of other planets in the universe, and some will have conditions similar to those on Earth. Perhaps they will be home to other types of life. Planets outside our solar system are too far away to visit, but astronomers search for signs that something might live on them. Living things on Earth change the atmosphere here, and our activity leaks radio signals into space. We look for similar signs of life on other planets. Perhaps we will be the first species on Earth to discover, and perhaps even contact, life on another planet or moon somewhere.

VIRTUAL WORLDS

The powerful machinery of the Industrial Revolution changed forever how physical work is carried out. Tasks that could never have been achieved with just the power of our muscles became possible, and other tasks became faster and more efficient. The computer revolution of the twentieth and twenty-first centuries did the same for mental work. A computer can sift, sort, and calculate more data in a few seconds than an individual could process in years. Computers are now central to all areas of our work lives and leisure.

Getting started

The English inventor Charles Babbage first tried to build a computer in the 1820s. With the help of Ada Lovelace, who wrote the instructions for his computer to follow, Babbage planned to automate the complicated and repetitive calculations needed in business and shipping. Practical and personal difficulties prevented his computers being built in his lifetime. But his aim—to free people from the need to repeat boring mental work—lived on. Computers were finally built more than 100 years later. They started as huge machines that filled rooms, but by the 1970s the technology to make them much smaller had been invented.

Colossus computer used for code-breaking in World War II.

Beyond brains

Computers are not intelligent and can't think for themselves. Their value lies in being able to work very quickly and accurately with huge amounts of data. They can only follow instructions in their programs, so humans still need to know how to do the work in order to write the programs. Tasks such as space travel involve more calculations than could be accomplished in a whole lifetime without computers. These tasks would not be possible without modern computers. Computers have stretched what humans can do beyond anything our ancestors could have imagined.

Computers helped us make vaccines during the Covid-19 pandemic that started in 2020.

With smartphones, we always have access to information from around the world.

Virtual lives

With the development of the world wide web in the 1990s, people can share information instantly, transforming how we live. Using computers, we can control machinery at a distance, perform surgery with a robot, or drive a rover over the surface of Mars. Just 200 years ago, to get a message from England to China took months. It would have been carried by land and sea, and would have been just text and perhaps a drawing or painting—no photos, video, or sound files. Now we can see and speak to each other from opposite sides of the world, and we can send enough information to fill an encyclopaedia in less than a second. We and our world have been transformed.

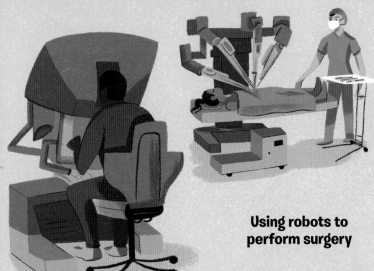

Using robots to perform surgery

Sustainable living is the exciting challenge of keeping living standards high while using fewer resources and protecting the environment.

A change of air

The Industrial Revolution was powered by burning fossils fuels—coal, then oil and gas. These formed from long-dead trees, plants, and microorganisms that locked away carbon from the atmosphere millions of years ago. When we burn them, that carbon returns to the atmosphere as carbon dioxide. The level of carbon dioxide in the air has risen by half since 1750. Increasing carbon dioxide and other greenhouse gases makes the world warmer. Warmer air leads to extreme weather events producing droughts, floods, wildfires, and hurricanes. Ice melts and sea levels rise, flooding low-lying areas.

Floods, caused by rising sea levels

Droughts

SAVING THE PLANET, SAVING OURSELVES

Humans have changed the planet for thousands of years. We have cleared the land with fire, diverted rivers, even changed the bodies of the animals and plants we domesticated. Change on a truly massive scale began with the Industrial Revolution, and now all parts of the world have been affected—usually badly—by us being here.

We are not alone

We depend on all the other living things on the planet. Yet we build on or pollute the places they live, and we kill them or their food supply directly with pesticides. In some countries, biodiversity (the variety of living things) is now half the level it was before the Industrial Revolution. Removing biodiversity threatens our own survival.

Back from the brink?

Civilization is at risk from its own success. But humans are intelligent. We have many skills and can use the most sophisticated tools ever made. We should be able to stop damaging the planet and ourselves. If we use renewable sources of energy that don't produce greenhouse gases, if we protect the other species we share the planet with, and if we stop destroying our environment, we can halt the damage. We will all have to adjust how we live—especially those of us in rich countries—and learn to protect our planet and our fellow beings. If we do that, we can flourish, and the story of humans can continue long into the future.

Chemicals to go

Since the Industrial Revolution, factories have made more and more goods—many of them things we don't really need. Making these produces waste that is poured into the environment. Some resources aren't renewable—once they are gone, there will be no more. The plastics we make from oil don't break down. They collect in the environment, causing harm.

Wildfires

117

TIMELINE I
THE PATH TO HUMANKIND

Earth formed in the new solar system.

Bacteria able to photosynthesize began to release oxygen. They produced so much that a catastrophic "Great Oxygenation Event" changed the composition of the sea and atmosphere, poisoning many microbes.

The Cambrian Explosion saw much more variety in living things. Some animals developed hard outsides, began to move, gained eyes, and began to eat one another. Everything still lived in the sea.

The first known tsexually reproducing organism was a type of red alga, called *Bangiomorpha*.

The first living things developed on Earth, microbes of a type that no longer exists.

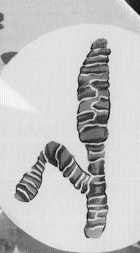

Life became more diverse, with larger organisms evolving, including the first animals living on the seabed.

HADEAN	End of Hadean	ARCHEAN	PROTEROZOIC		End of Proterozoic
4.55 billion years ago	4.5–3.7 billion years ago	3.6–2.7 billion years ago	1047 million years ago	570 million years ago	540 million years ago

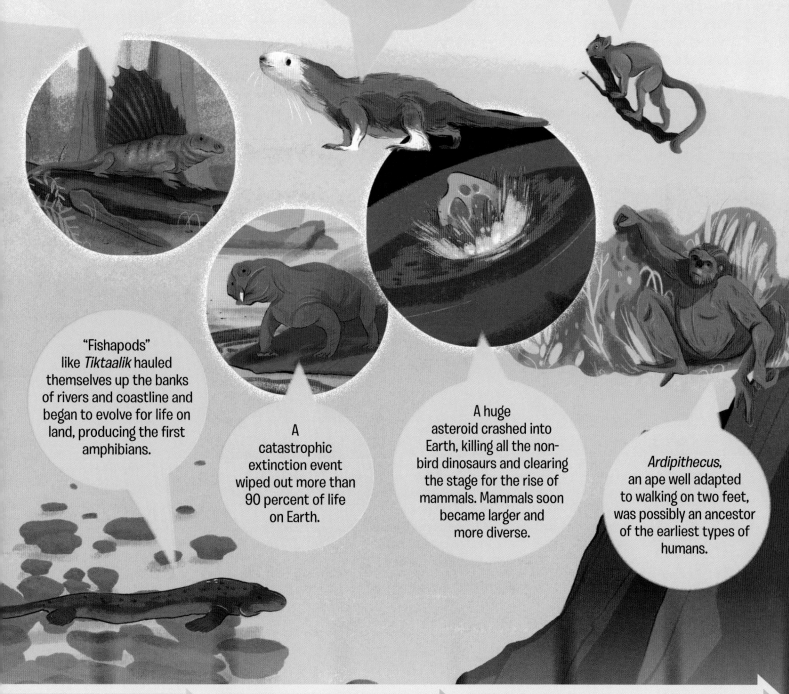

From amphibians, reptiles evolved that could live anywhere on land, laying eggs that didn't dry out. Some of these reptiles developed features that later mammals would keep.

After the catastrophe, the first mammals appeared, small furry animals that probably came out at night and lived in the trees and burrows, eating insects.

The first primate, *Archicebus*, was about the size of a mouse. It lived in trees and shared features with later monkeys.

"Fishapods" like *Tiktaalik* hauled themselves up the banks of rivers and coastline and began to evolve for life on land, producing the first amphibians.

A catastrophic extinction event wiped out more than 90 percent of life on Earth.

A huge asteroid crashed into Earth, killing all the non-bird dinosaurs and clearing the stage for the rise of mammals. Mammals soon became larger and more diverse.

Ardipithecus, an ape well adapted to walking on two feet, was possibly an ancestor of the earliest types of humans.

PHANEROZOIC	Paleozoic	Mesozoic		Cenozoic		
375 million years ago	295 million years ago	252 million years ago	225 million years ago	65.5 million years ago	55 million years ago	7–4 million years ago

TIMELINE 2
THE RISE OF HUMANKIND

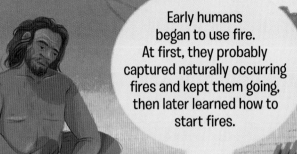

The first stone tools were made by some unknown type of early human.

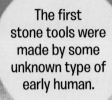

Early humans began to use fire. At first, they probably captured naturally occurring fires and kept them going, then later learned how to start fires.

Early humans, probably Neanderthals, made shelters from sticks, reeds, or grasses in Europe.

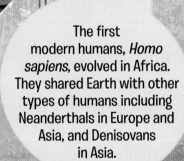

Homo habilis was the first species of human known to make and use tools.

Homo erectus was the first species of human to leave Africa and begin to spread around the world.

The first modern humans, *Homo sapiens*, evolved in Africa. They shared Earth with other types of humans including Neanderthals in Europe and Asia, and Denisovans in Asia.

Cenozoic

| 2.6 million years ago | 2.4 million years ago | 2 million years ago | 1.5 million –790,000 years ago | 380,000 years ago | 315,000–300,000 years ago |

The latest ice age (or glacial period) plunged Europe, Northern Russia, and North America into freezing temperatures. Humans could survive by using fire and dressing in the pelts of animals they hunted.

People made bone sewing needles to fashion clothes from skins or fabrics.

In some parts of the world, people began to settle into stable communities and farm the land, growing crops and keeping animals for meat.

Homo sapiens began their slow journey from Africa to cover the whole planet, except for Antarctica.

Neanderthals in Europe left the first cave paintings.

People began to domesticate wolves, turning them into dogs. They were probably first used as hunting companions and for protection, but soon also used to round up goats or sheep.

| 115,000–12,000 years ago | 100,000 years ago | 66,700 years ago | 35,000 years ago | 20,000 years ago | 12,000 years ago |

TIMELINE 3
CIVILIZATION DAWNS

People domesticated plants and animals, changing them by selectively planting and breeding those that had the features people valued.

The first municipal city with public spaces and a civic structure was Sumer, which grew up in an area that is now Iraq.

Sumerians began writing by pressing characters into a clay tablet.

From 14,000 years ago, we begin to use dates BCE (before the Common Era) and CE (Common Era); 14,000 years ago is 12,000 BCE.

Çatalhöyük, now in Turkey, was the first city, with a population of around 5,000–7,000 people.

People began to work with metal, making first bronze and later iron tools and weapons. This happened at different times in different places, starting in Europe and the Middle East.

14,000 years ago	11,000 BCE	7500–6400 BCE	4500 BCE	4000 BCE	3300 BCE

The Ancient Egyptians started building pyramids to hold the bodies of dead pharaohs and other nobles.

The Harappan civilization of the Indus Valley in present-day Pakistan had an advanced system of plumbing and water management, the first in the world.

Stonehenge in England was used as a huge calendar, tracking the position of sunrise around the year.

The earliest written legal code was recorded Hammurabi.

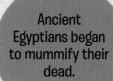

Polynesian sailors set out into the South China Sea and later the Pacific Ocean, populating islands across vast tracts of sea over thousands of years.

Ancient Egyptians began to mummify their dead.

The story of Gilgamesh was written down in Sumerian, the language used in Sumer. It is the oldest surviving written story.

The Olmec were the first known major civilization in South America.

| 3000 BCE | 2600 BCE | 2575–2150 BCE | 2400 BCE | 2000 BCE | 1750 BCE | 1200–400 BCE |

TIMELINE 4
CONNECTING THE WORLD

594 BCE
Athens (in Greece) and the first form of democratic government, giving all adult free men say in how the city was governed.

130 CE
Connections between East and West grew, with routes opening overland and then by sea between Europe, the Middle East, Africa, India, and China.

1344–1353 CE
A devastating plague, the Black Death, swept through Asia, North Africa and Europe killing up to half the population in affected areas.

221 BCE
Qin Shi Huang united much of China, starting an empire that would last 2,000 years.

1206–1279 CE
The Mongolian empire stretched from Mongolia (between China and Russia) to Hungary in Europe—the largest continuous land empire there has ever been.

762–1258 CE
The House of Wisdom in Baghdad allowed for learning from previous civilizations in Europe, Africa, and Asia.

1439 CE
The invention of the printing press meant that books could be easily and quickly produced. More people began to read, and new scientific discoveries could quickly spread around the world, beginning the modern era of shared knowledge.

100 BCE   100 CE   1000 CE   1500 CE

1600s–1865 CE
Millions of people were enslaved and forcibly shipped from Africa to work in the Americas and the West Indies.

1914–1918 CE
World War I saw the devastation of Western Europe and the slaughter of millions around the world.

1939–1945 CE
World War II raged around the world, killing 70–85 million people. War was a spur to invention, bringing the first working computer as well as better planes, radar, and the first atomic bombs.

1991 CE–present
The development of the worldwide web and widespread use of computers has changed how we live and how we interact with others, providing instant communications all across the world.

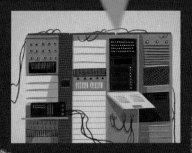

1760–1840 CE
The Industrial Revolution began the age of mass transportation and mechanized factories —and the large-scale use of fossil fuels. People moved into cities, and goods went from being hand-produced to made largely by machines.

1919–1921 CE
A global flu pandemic killed 50–100 million people worldwide.

1957 CE
Space travel took humans and their robotic craft beyond Earth to explore the solar system.

1980s CE –present
The effects of climate change caused by human activity begin to emerge. Climate change threatens land and lives unless we change how we live to be more sustainable.

1600 CE   **1900 CE**   **2000 CE**

125

GLOSSARY

abstract Not relating to physical objects, but to ideas and concepts.

agriculture Farming.

amphibian An animal that has smooth, moist skin and must lay its eggs in water. The larval (young) form looks different from the adult form and lives in water and takes oxygen from the water, while the adult breathes air.

anesthetic A medicine that blocks pain, numbing an area or putting a patient to sleep.

ancestor An organism from which another is descended, several or many generations back.

antiseptic A chemical or medicine that prevents the growth of bacteria or other microbes that could cause infection or illness.

archea A simple type of microbe (organism with one cell) that first appeared on Earth billions of years ago.

astronomy The scientific study of space and everything in it.

atmosphere The layer of gas around a planet.

bacteria Simple microbes (organisms with one cell) that are found all over Earth in many different environments. They first appeared on Earth billions of years ago.

caliph The religious and political ruler in an Islamic state, considered the successor to the prophet Muhammad.

chromosome A strand of the chemical DNA which holds some of an organism's genetic information in the form of a chemical code.

civilian A person who is not in the military (so not a soldier, or other member of the army, navy, or air force).

civilization A complex social structure in which people live and work together with rules and roles to support the group's survival.

climate Long-term patterns of weather and temperature.

coptic Belonging or relating to a part of the Christian Church, which was started in Egypt in the third century CE.

Crusades Military campaigns undertaken by medieval Christians with the stated aim of seizing places considered holy to Christianity. They often involved looting, massacres, and other abuse.

democratic Allowing the people to express their views and elect (choose) people to represent them and make laws for them.

dictator A ruler who has a great deal of power, often seized illegally.

domesticate To tame and often change the features of a plant or animal to suit human uses.

ecosystem A system of organisms and their environment.

enslaved Treated as an item of property and forced to work without pay or choices.

environment The natural setting of land, water, or another place where an organism lives.

eruption An outpouring of lava, gases, smoke, and ash from a volcano.

evolve To change form over several generations, often adapting to changes in the environment where an organism lives.

famine An extreme shortage of food, leading people to starve.

fertile Rich and full of nourishment for plants.

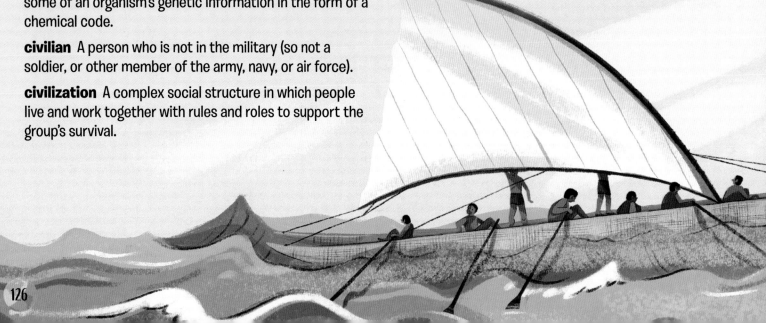

fired Heated at a very high temperature to become hard.

genetic Relating to inherited characteristics.

gully A channel in the ground.

halaf Of or belonging to the prehistoric period that lasted between about 6100 BCE and 5100 BCE in northern Mesopotamia and Syria.

import An item brought into a country from elsewhere for sale.

impoverished Made poor.

indentured Having agreed to work for someone for a long time, for a fixed price.

Industrial Revolution The period when many manufacturing and farming tasks became mechanized (carried out by machines), factories were built, and steam engines were widely used to power machinery and vehicles.

interstellar Between the stars.

linen A fabric made from fibers of the plant flax.

literature A body of written works such as poetry, novels, essays, and plays.

megafauna Very large land animals.

microbe An organism with a single cell.

migrate Move from one place to another.

Minoan Relating to the early civilization on the Greek island of Crete.

monopoly Complete control of the market for a particular type of item or service.

mosaic A picture made up of lots of tiny parts.

multicelled An organism with with more than one cell.

municipal Relating to a town and how it is governed.

mya Millions of years ago.

Old World Parts of the world that were connected by transport links before 1550: Europe, Asia, and Africa.

organism A living thing.

papyrus Material for writing on made from the fibers of the papyrus reed.

pesticide A chemical used to kill animals considered pests, such as insects.

pharaoh A ruler in ancient Egypt.

photosynthesize To use sunlight to breakdown carbon dioxide and water, producing glucose (a sugar) and oxygen.

primate Member of the group of mammals that includes monkeys and apes, including humans.

quipu Object made of knotted threads used by the Incas of South America to record numbers and probably words.

radiation Energy in the form of electromagnetic waves that can have many different sources.

refugee A person who has had to leave their home because of terrible circumstances, such as war or a natural disaster.

resources Useful supplies, such as food, water, fuel, and building materials.

sediment Sand, mud, or bits of plant matter that settle out of water.

smelt To heat rock that contains metal to melt the metal and extract it.

tempered Heated in a fire to make harder or stronger.

textile Fabric.

vaccination A small dose of a disease-causing microbe that has been made safe, given to prompt the body to build immunity to the disease.

INDEX